Origami ZOO

25 Fun Paper Animal Creations

Paul Jackson and Miri Golan

Illustrations by Paul Jackson
Photographs by Avi Valdman

D0752057

GIBBS SMITH
TO ENRICH AND INSPIRE HUMANKIND

Dedicated to
Kunihiko Kasahara,
master creator of origami animals
and my first origami teacher. PJ

Dedicated to
Makoto Yamaguchi.
MG

First Edition
15 14 13 12 11   5 4 3 2 1

Text © 2011 Paul Jackson and Miri Golan
Illustrations © 2011 Paul Jackson
Photographs © 2011 Avi Valdman

Published by
Gibbs Smith
P.O. Box 667
Layton, Utah 84041

1.800.835.4993 orders
www.gibbs-smith.com

Designed by Kurt Wahlner
Manufactured in Shenzhen, China, in December 2010 by Toppan Printing

Gibbs Smith books are printed on either recycled, 100% post-consumer
waste, FSC-certified papers or on paper produced from sustainable PEFC-
certified forest/controlled wood source. Learn more at www.pefc.org.

Library of Congress Cataloging-in-Publication Data

Jackson, Paul, 1956-
  Origami zoo : 25 fun paper animal creations / Paul Jackson and Miri Golan ;
illustrations by Paul Jackson ; photographs by Avi Valdman. — 1st ed.
    p. cm.
  ISBN 978-1-4236-2016-7
  1. Origami. 2. Animals in art. I. Golan, Miri. II. Title.
  TT870.J3225 2011
  736'.982—dc22
                        2010040524

Contents

Acknowledgments

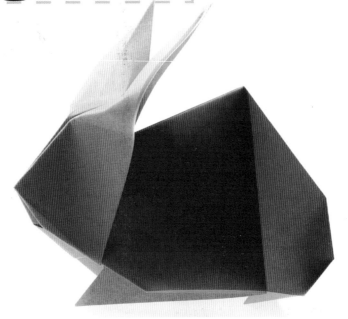

Paul writes: My thanks are due to the many origami creators who have influenced my style of folding, in particular Kunihiko Kasahara (to whom the book is part dedicated) and other Japanese creators of the classical style, including Toshie Takahama, Makoto Yamaguchi and the origami artists of the Nippon Origami Association; also Eric Kennaway and other creators for whom the total look of an origami design is more important than its detail. I must also sincerely thank my wife, Miri Golan, for designing the book's many splendidly clear folding sequences, and for her support and encouragement throughout the preparation of the manuscript.

Miri writes: My thanks are due to all my students who, through my many mistakes, have taught me the best way to teach; to Dr. Dina Vardi, who has inspired me over many years; to Paul for widening my origami world; and to our son, Jonathan, whose enthusiasm for origami gave me insights I would not otherwise have had, especially regarding the importance of preschool origami.

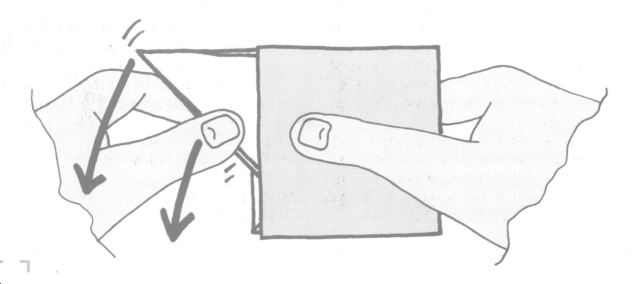

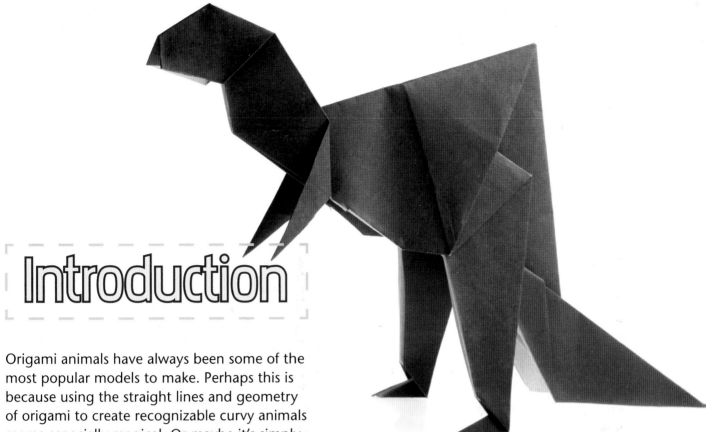

Introduction

Origami animals have always been some of the most popular models to make. Perhaps this is because using the straight lines and geometry of origami to create recognizable curvy animals seems especially magical. Or maybe it's simply because we all love animals!

Folding origami animals brings its own challenges. Many of the models in the book require you to use your own judgment when making some of the folds. Make a fold in the wrong place and a head can become too large, or a leg can become too short, and your finished model can look misshapen. So, regard your first attempt at folding a new model as a folded "sketch," learning the placement of the folds and perhaps repositioning them a few times until your "sketch" looks good. Then, take a fresh sheet of paper and fold it right. Remember: origami animals are essentially cartoons—a simplification of a complex form—so take time to learn exactly where each of the folds should be placed. Think of yourself as a musician learning a new piece of music; at first you play the notes mechanically, but when you know the piece, you can play the music accurately and with expression.

The models have been arranged in approximately the order of difficulty. If you are new to origami or have only a little experience, you are encouraged to start at the beginning. Jumping in too deep, too early, can be very frustrating.

Most of the models are my own creations, some dating back more than thirty years. Three models have been created by my wife, Miri Golan, and one by our son, Jonathan, when he was five years old. Just use your imagination to play with the paper as Jonathan often does, and you will soon be creating your own masterpieces.

The step-by-step folding sequences were created by Miri, a professional origami educator who has twenty years of experience and is widely regarded as the foremost authority on origami in education. Her instruction style—a result of thousands of hours of teaching origami to children and adults of all abilities—is the clearest I have seen, and her important contribution to the book fully justifies her title as co-author.

Just as this book has been a family production, we hope you'll share the models inside with your own family and help spread the joy of origami through the generations.

We wish you happy folding!

Paul Jackson
Miri Golan

Read This!

If you are new to origami or if it has been some years since you picked up an origami book, please read this introductory chapter. Instead of trying to fold the most complicated models in the book without perhaps knowing the difference between a valley fold and a mountain fold, I encourage you to read carefully through these pages. They will help you to enjoy your folding more and help ensure your success.

Paper

The absolute best paper to use for most of the models in this book is specialist origami paper. Origami paper is square paper, colored on one side and white on the other, a little thinner than common photocopier paper. The difference in color between the two sides is often used to improve the recognition of a model—for example, by creating different-colored eyes—rather than being used to prettify a model. Thus, the color change is often functional rather than merely decorative.

Origami paper can be bought from a number of sources:

1. Stores. Try toy stores, Japanese and East Asian stores, art and craft stores, stationery stores, and office supply stores.

2. Origami societies. Most Western countries have an organized origami society that will sell origami paper (and books and more). To find the one local to you, simply type "origami" and your country name into an online search engine.

3. Online. Entering "origami paper" into a search engine will bring up many online retailers. You could also try auction sites for a bargain.

If you have a problem obtaining origami paper, use copier paper. This is an excellent paper for folding, inexpensive and readily available. The drawback is that it has the same color on both sides, but this might be considered only a minor disadvantage. Office supply stores will sell copier paper not only in white (how boring!), but also in a variety of colors, sometimes mixing a selection of colors together in a packet.

If you are buying a large quantity of copier paper, consider asking a walk-in print and copy shop to cut it accurately square on an electric guillotine, thus saving you the labor of cutting every rectangle individually to a square, or worse, to an almost square. This quick service should be inexpensive.

For those impromptu moments when you are seized by the urge to fold, or when someone suddenly requests you fold that amazing model you made last week, other papers are also suitable for folding. Try using printed junk mail—a wonderful free source of excellent paper—or magazines, old photocopies, or notepads. In truth, most papers that are printed on are okay to fold and the potential for recycling and reusing papers in this way makes great sense in this age of increasing green awareness. Indeed, I know of origami people who, on principle, never buy paper to fold—they reuse papers of all kinds that others have discarded. Good for them.

Papers to avoid include newspapers, paper towels, tissue and any other paper that will not hold a crease well.

Most origami books will rightly encourage you to fold your favorite origami models from beautiful papers and exhibit them for everyone to admire. However, the animal models in this book will look great made from the paper supplied with the book, or with another two-tone origami paper. But if you are making models to exhibit, then it is worthwhile to visit art and craft stores to see what extra-special papers you can find. If you live in a major city, it may well have a specialist paper store, full of amazing types of paper. A telephone directory, business directory or an Internet search will soon locate such a store.

Folding Tips

Create a Good Environment

There's nothing to stop you folding on your lap in front of the TV, your phone locked to your ear and the cat sitting on your head . . . but you can and should create a better environment in which to fold.

1. Sit at a table. Fold on a hard, smooth, clean surface. If a table is not available or if you are infirm, a large hardback book is a good substitute.

2. Good light. Try to organize your seating arrangement so that the light is coming towards you from the front, not from directly overhead or from the sides. A frontal light source will create shadows across the folds of your paper, helping you to fold with greater accuracy and fluency. Try switching lights on or off, moving your chair, or even going to another room. Natural daylight through a window is a better source than artificial lighting. Good light is not an optional luxury, but a necessity.

3. Your own zone. Turn off your phone, switch off the TV, put the cat out and do whatever you need to do to be able to focus on your folding. This is your time to enjoy yourself. We all need time to "center" ourselves, and doing origami is a wonderful way to achieve this.

Following the Drawings in the Book

Origami drawings are a language unto themselves. To fold successfully, you need to understand the instructions. Here are some tips and tricks:

1. The symbols. Try to learn them! When you are folding and you see a symbol you don't understand, refer to the Symbols table on pages 9–10.

2. Look ahead. The symbols on one step will create a paper shape that looks like the next step, but is stripped of its new symbols. So, to see the result of what you are folding on any current step, look ahead to the next step. In this way, a sequence of drawings can be thought of as a chain of interconnected links, not a series of unrelated, self-contained steps.

3. Fold slowly. Take your time. Don't rush. Enjoy the process of folding. You are not in a race.

4. Fold carefully. What one person may consider careful folding, another may consider unacceptably sloppy or unnecessarily precise, so the best advice is to fold as best you can. Origami animals are best folded precisely, but if you are overly worried by the accuracy of what you are folding, just do what is within your capability. If precision is a problem, with practice, it will improve.

5. Try again. From time to time, we all become stuck. To unstick yourself, first try unfolding a few steps to a point where you are sure everything is correct, then folding forwards again. Maybe you made a mistake somewhere and refolding the last few steps will solve the problem. Second, as mentioned above, look ahead to the next step to see the shape that you are trying to achieve. Third, if you are still stuck, put your paper down, do something else, and try again later. This often works! Remember, though, that making origami from a book is always a challenge and the learning curve for some people can sometimes appear steep, so an attitude of patience and cheerful perseverance is most helpful (and not just for origami!).

Folding Your Paper

There are good and not so good ways to fold. Following a few simple guidelines will make your folding experience more pleasurable.

1. Fold away from you. When making a fold, always pick up an edge or corner near to you and fold it away from your body, making the new crease on the edge of the paper nearest to your body. Never do the opposite: never pull an edge or corner far away from you towards your body and crease across the top of the paper. Thus, you must constantly rotate the paper so that for every new fold the paper is correctly positioned. Rotate, rotate, rotate!

2. Fold on a surface or in the air? It is sometimes better to fold against a hard surface and sometimes better to fold in the air between your hands . . . but when and why? Generally, make long creases against a surface; they will be made more accurately. This usually means all the early folds. Later, when the main folds have been put in, pick up the paper and work with it between your hands. Experts like to fold entirely in the air (the "ballet of the paper" and all that), but it is better for beginners and intermediates to fold against a surface.

It is worth remembering that origami is not just a folded art, but a folding art; that is, the process of folding should be enjoyable, not just a means to an end, to be rushed though as quickly as possible on the way to making a model. Think of folding as a gourmet meal, whose delicate and diverse flavors and

many courses should be savored slowly. Folding should not be like gobbling down drive-through fast food and speeding off. Following the above advice will make your folding experience pleasurable, not a chore, and you will want to do more. The art of origami should be a sensory experience, never just a mechanical means to an end.

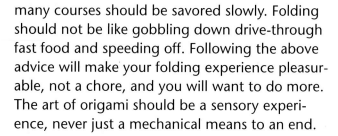

What to Do with Your Origami Animals

In two words, share them!

Origami models should be shared. Learn a few of your favorites by heart and make them for family and friends, or as icebreakers with strangers at parties, dreary meetings, long flights and the like. A designer friend once told me how she traveled from remote village to remote village in several Southeast Asian countries on a research project, gaining the friendship and help of the villagers by folding origami models for everyone!

If you have the confidence, teach the models to club groups, young or old. Origami animals are great to teach to children, who love to play with them. Adults too love to make animals. Some of my most enjoyable workshops have been with groups as diverse as MA graphic design students at design college in central London, a group of engineering professionals, a group of elderly ladies at a day center, and a small class of children at a rural village deep in the English countryside. Teaching origami is always fun.

If you are a teacher, teach origami animals in class as a fun end-of-semester treat, or more seriously in math, science, and technology classes (there are some great examples of geometry contained in the models). Teaching models to disruptive children gives them status and self-confidence, or models can be given as rewards for good behavior. I know of therapists who gain the trust of children by making origami for them and who use models in role-playing games.

The essence of origami is its innocent delight. But presented in the right way at the right time, it may also have a serious educational or therapeutic use. Don't confuse fun with triviality!

Symbols

It's not so much the step-by-step drawings themselves as the symbols superimposed on them that tell you how to make an origami model. Over the years, a general consensus has been unofficially agreed between origami authors of many countries and different languages to make the symbols universal. This means (in theory, anyway) that paper folders around the world can pick up any origami book and be able to make the models it contains because the symbols are broadly the same, book to book and language to language. The symbols included in this book are not the complete set used worldwide, but are sufficient to enable you to make the models it contains.

With two exceptions, the symbols are largely self-explanatory. The exceptions are the symbols for the two basic folds of valley fold and mountain fold (actually, if you think about it, they are the same fold). The symbols for each should be learned before you begin the book.

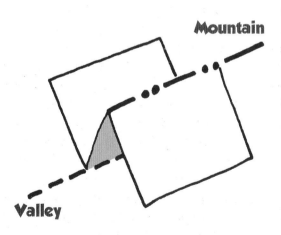

Valley fold

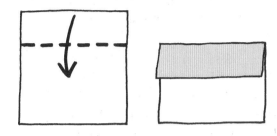

Mountain fold

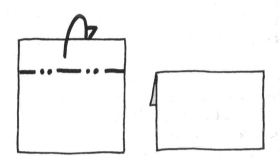

Existing fold

Fold and open

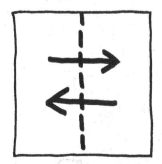

X-ray view or tuck in

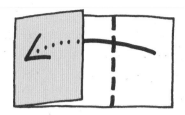

Turn over

Fold dot to dot

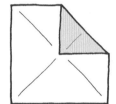

Techniques

Valley folds and mountain folds are simply "folds." That is, one new fold is made at a time, either by bringing part of the paper towards you (to make a valley fold) or turning it away from you (to make a mountain fold), then flattening it to make a new crease. That's really all there is to say about valley-mountain folding. Making these basic folds couldn't be simpler.

However, there are more complex techniques in which a number of new folds are made simultaneously. These techniques are important because they hugely increase the possible number of folded shapes and thus, they increase perhaps almost to infinity the number of models that can be made.

There are many advanced manipulation techniques (Squash, Sink, Rabbit Ear, Petal Fold, etc.) but the most common techniques are the Inside Reverse Fold and its less common complement, the Outside Reverse Fold. Once learned, they are very quick and simple to make, but at first sight they can seem difficult to understand. If you are unfamiliar with these techniques, I strongly recommend you make the examples that follow, rather than fold them for the first time when folding a model.

Inside Reverse Fold

This is so called because the part of the paper that is manipulated reverses inside the remainder of the paper.

1. Begin with a square, white side up. Fold in half along a diagonal and unfold.

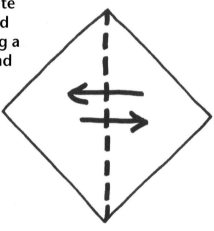

2. Fold the top left and top right edges to the center line.

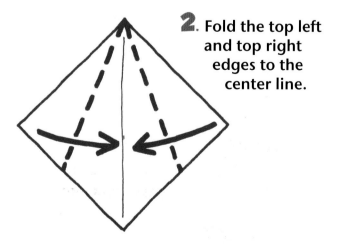

3. Fold in half along the Step 1 crease.

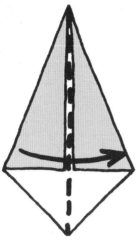

7. Along the same crease line just made, now make a mountain fold, bending the sharp corner behind.

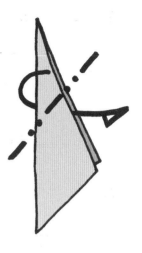

4. Fold the sharp corner across to the right, to the position shown in Step 5. The exact position is unimportant.

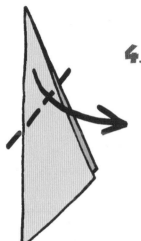

8. Unfold. The crease can now fold forwards or backwards.

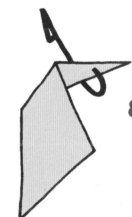

5. Unfold.

9. Unfold the Step 1 center crease.

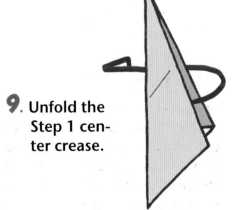

6. This is how the paper will look.

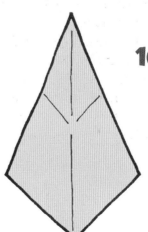

10. This is the pattern of folds. Note the "V" in the center.

11. Think of the paper as having four folds that all meet at the bottom of the "V." From this side of the paper, three of those folds will be mountains, and one will be a valley. If you make these four folds one at a time and then collapse all the creases simultaneously, you can jump straight to the end, at Step 16, but it is more instructive to follow the method in Steps 12–15.

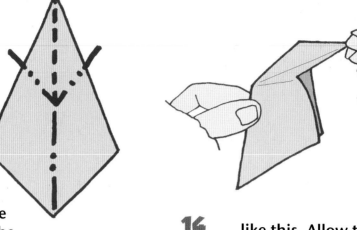

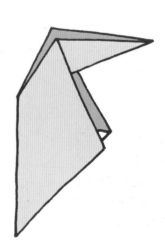

14. . . . like this. Allow the "V" fold to form. Make the valley fold seen in Step 11, so that the paper will begin to flatten itself . . .

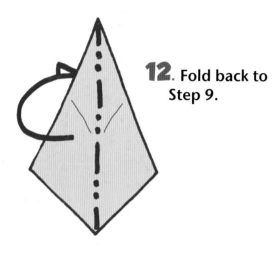

12. Fold back to Step 9.

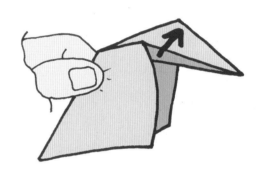

15. . . . like this. Continue to flatten the paper . . .

13. Hold the paper as shown between your two hands. Begin to move the sharp corner downwards and—crucially—down through the middle of the paper, between the front and back sides . . .

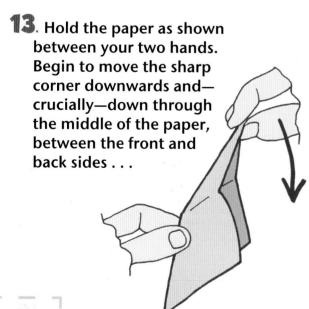

16. . . . until the Inside Reverse Fold is complete.

Inside Reverse Folds in the Book

The explanation above took many steps, too many to be repeated again and again in the book. So, here is how the book explains what you have just done.

Make an inside reverse fold.

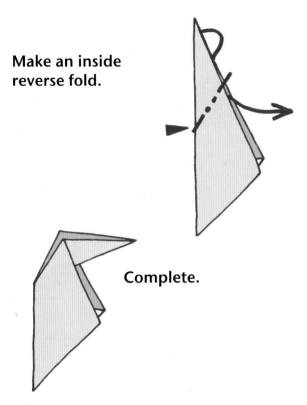

Complete.

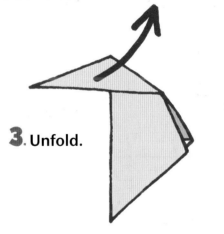

2. Bend the sharp corner out to the left. This is in the opposite direction as it is when making an Inside Reverse Fold.

3. Unfold.

Outside Reverse Fold

This is so called because the part of the paper that is manipulated reverses outside the remainder of the paper.

1. Begin with Step 4 of the Inside Reverse Fold, but without the new fold made on that step.

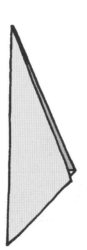

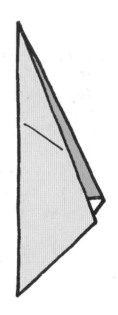

4. This is how the paper will look.

5. Along the same crease line just made, now make a mountain fold, bending the sharp corner behind.

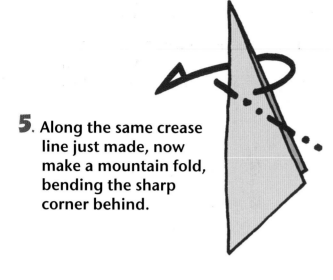

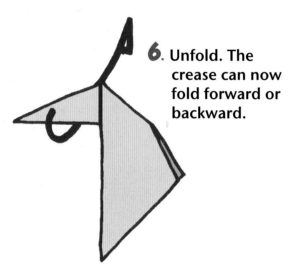

6. Unfold. The crease can now fold forward or backward.

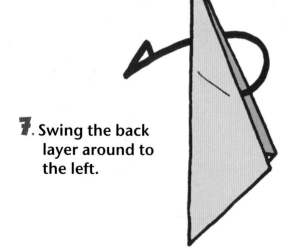

7. Swing the back layer around to the left.

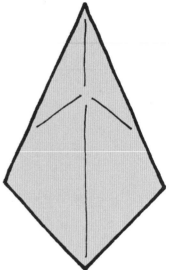

8. This is the pattern of folds. Note the upturned "V" in the center. Note too how this pattern differs from the Inside Reverse Fold.

9. Think of the paper as having four folds that all meet at the top of the upturned "V." From this side of the paper, three of those folds will be valleys and one will be a mountain. Note how the number of valleys and mountains is reversed, compared to the Inside Reverse Fold. If you make these four folds one at a time and then collapse all the creases simultaneously, you can jump straight to the end, at Step 12, but it is more instructive to follow the method in Steps 10–11.

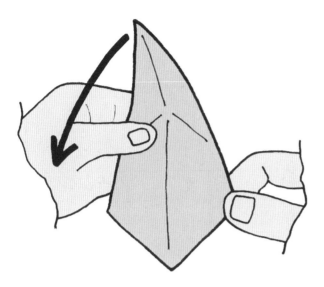

Outside Reverse Folds in the Book

The explanation above took many steps, too many to be repeated again and again in the book. So, here is how the book explains what you have just done.

Make an outside reverse fold.

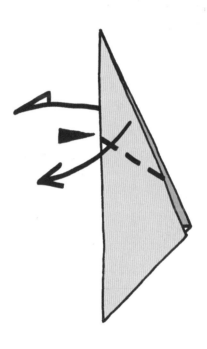

10. Hold the paper as shown. Bend the sharp corner forward, simultaneously folding the paper in half down the middle and allowing the valley folds of the upturned "V" to form . . .

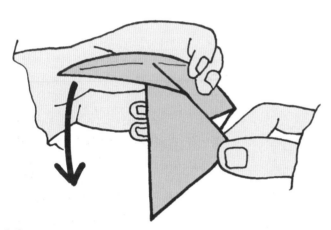

11. . . . like this. For a while the paper will be curvy, so encourage it to flatten . . .

Complete.

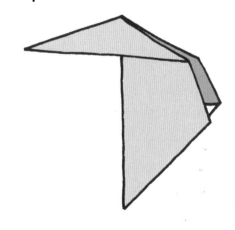

12. . . . until the Outside Reverse Fold is complete.

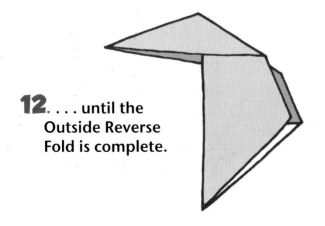

Koala

Here is an example of extreme simplification in origami design. Just four simple valley folds are enough to conjure the likeness of a koala from the paper—who would have thought it?! And yet, for all its simplicity, it is also rather subtle; the folds in steps 2 and 3 need to be made with accuracy or the koala becomes unrecognizable.

Begin with a square of paper, koala colored on one side.

1. White side up, fold down the middle, bringing the right edge across to the left edge.

2. Fold dot to dot. Note that the fold starts at the top right-hand corner of the paper and finishes a little above the bottom left-hand corner . . .

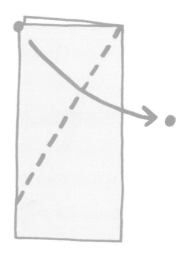

16

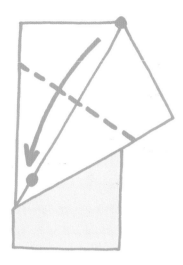

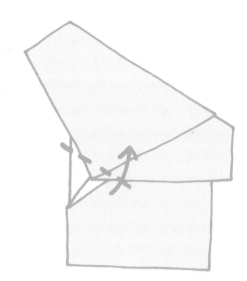

3. . . . like this. Fold dot to dot. Note that the lower dot is not on the edge of the paper, but a little way inside, exactly on the Step 2 fold.

4. Fold back the corner just a little way, to create a white nose.

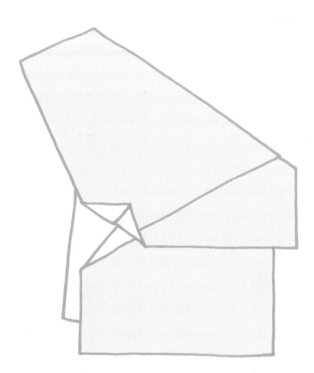

5. The Koala complete.

Penguin

Penguins are a favorite origami subject and almost every origami creator has at least one. It is one of the few upright animals, which sometimes creates problems of balance if your folding is a little uneven.

Begin with a square of paper, black on one side.

1. White side up, fold in half down the middle, bringing the left corner across to the right corner. Unfold.

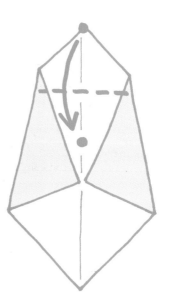

2. Fold the left and right corners to the center line. Notice how the middle dot is below the level of the other dots, so that the folds are not parallel to the center line, but taper inwards towards the top.

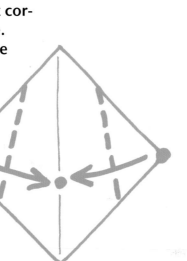

3. Fold down the top corner to a point a little way above the touching corners . . .

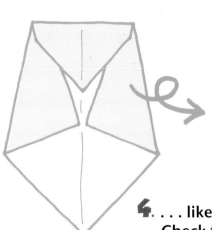

4. . . . like this. Check that what you have folded looks like the drawing, then turn the paper over.

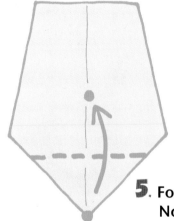

5. Fold dot to dot. Note that the fold is a little way below the left and right corners of the paper.

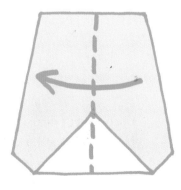

6. Fold in half, bringing the right edge across to the left edge.

7. With your left hand, hold the wings tightly shut. With your right hand, hold the head and swivel it upwards, so that the beak stands away from the paper . . .

8. . . . like this. The back of the head will now be curved, so press the paper flat to make new creases, being careful to do so with the beak in the correct position.

9. The Penguin complete.

Monster Puppet

Over the past few years, Miri has evolved a program of origami to help teach the basics of geometry to preschool children. One of the problems teaching origami to children of this age is their lack of accuracy, so she has created a series of models, including this one, that can be folded inaccurately by young hands but still look great.

Begin with a square of paper, monster colored on one side.

1. White side up, fold in half across the middle, bringing the top edge down to the bottom edge.

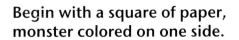

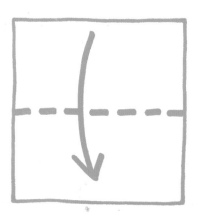

2. Fold in both layers of the bottom corners, but leave a space between the tops of the triangles and the top edge of the paper . . .

3. . . . like this. The exact shape and size of the triangles is unimportant. Turn the paper over.

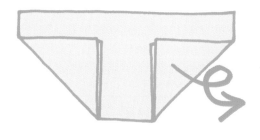

4. With sloping folds, turn in the top corners a little way . . .

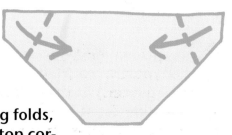

5. . . . like this. Again, the exact shape and size of what you fold is unimportant. Turn the paper over.

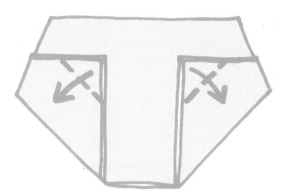

6. Left and right, fold down the front layer only, exposing white paper beneath.

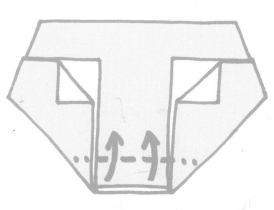

7. (This is an optional fold. You might want to omit it if you are teaching a young child or a beginner.) At the bottom edge, fold up the front layer only. Note how the left and right ends of the fold are hidden inside the cheeks . . .

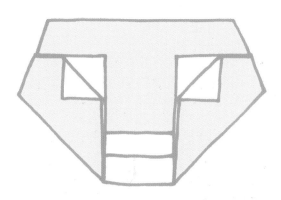

8. . . . like this. The folding is complete.

9. Insert a finger into the pocket . . . and play with your Monster Puppet!

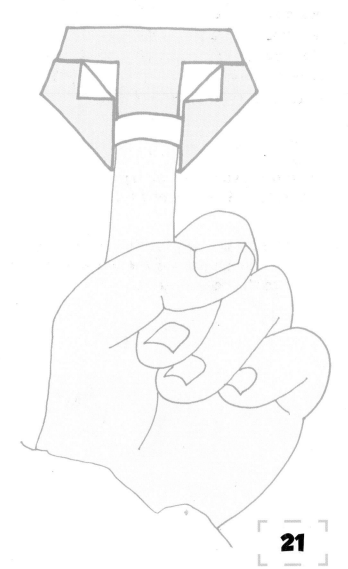

21

Mouse

Thinking simple, an origami mouse is essentially a triangular shape, wider at the head end than the tail, with a couple of extra triangles for ears at the head end. There are many ways to fold this simple shape, seen here in Step 10, and this is my way.

Begin with a square of paper, mouse colored on one side.

1. Color side up, fold the paper in half down the center, bringing the left corner across to the right corner. Unfold.

2. Similarly, now fold in half across the center.

3. The paper is now white. Fold the top corners down to the bottom corner.

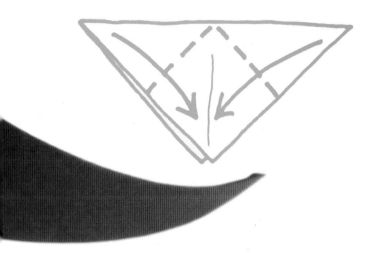

5. There are two layers at the bottom corner, one behind the other. Fold back the top layer only, just a little way.

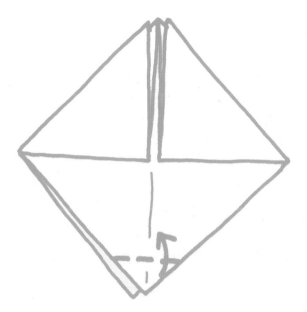

4. Fold the two loose corners at the bottom, up to the top corner.

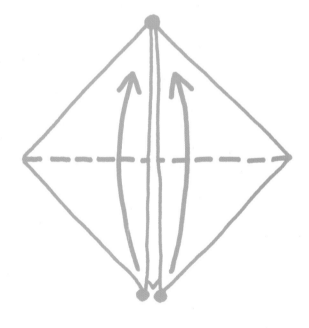

6. Now fold the same top layer up over the white triangles, to cover them . . .

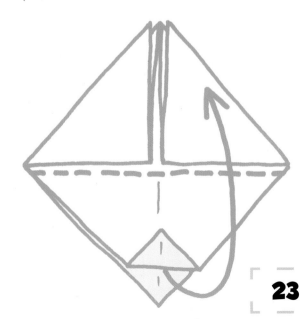

23

7. . . . like this. Note how most of the
   paper is now colored, with just two
   small white triangles showing at
   the top corner. Turn the paper over,
   keeping the white triangles at the
   top corner.

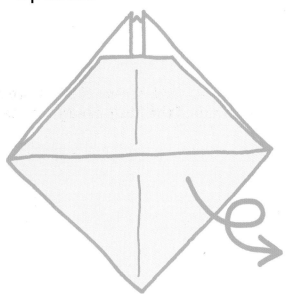

9. Fold in half down
   the center line . . .

8. Fold in the bottom left and bottom
   right edges of the paper to the center
   line. Much of the length of each fold
   is through only one layer of paper,
   but towards the top end, the paper
   suddenly becomes very thick and has
   to be folded flat with some strength.

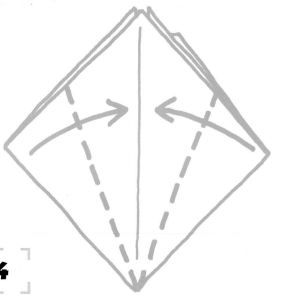

10. . . . like this.
   Rotate the paper
   to make it more
   mouse-like.

11. Fold back the two white triangles so that they stand away from the body.

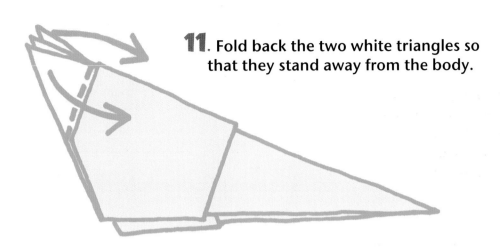

12. Fold the tail forward, so that the bottom edge of the tail is on top of the bottom edge of the body.

13. Using your fingers, curl the tail backwards to look like Step 14.

14. The Mouse complete.

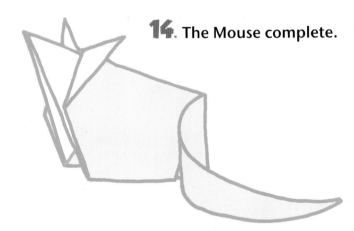

Sleepy Cow

This model includes a drawn element—the sleepy eye. Normally I don't like to see drawing on a model because it suggests that the folding is somehow incomplete. However, I believe the eye adds character here, so I've made an exception to my rule.

Begin with a square of paper, cow colored on one side.

1. White side up, fold in half across the middle, bringing the bottom corner up to the top corner. Unfold.

2. Bring the left corner across to the right corner, but instead of folding, make a small pinch in the middle of the paper. This will locate the center point of the sheet.

3. Fold the top and bottom corners to the center point of the paper. If your judgment is good, you can make these folds without making the Step 2 pinch.

4. Turn the paper over.

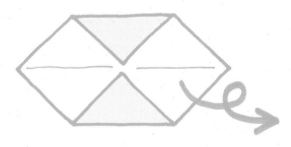

5. Step 6 shows an enlargement of the right-hand corner.

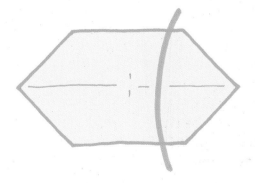

6. Fold the corner over twice, each time making very small folds. You might need to adjust these folds when the model is finished, so that they are the correct size.

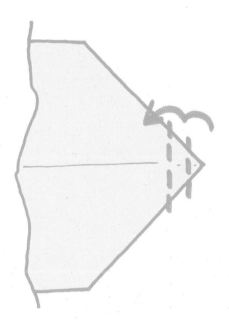

7. This is how the small folds should look.

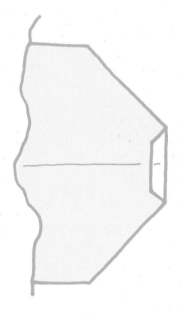

8. Turn the paper over.

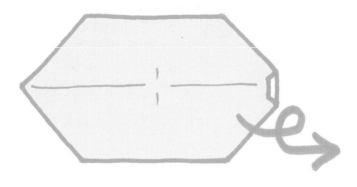

9. Fold the paper in half.

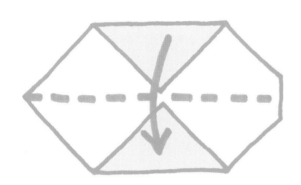

10. Fold down the corner . . .

11. . . . like this. Notice how the bottom edge of the head is parallel to the bottom of the paper. Fold dot to dot, so that the fold starts at the bottom left corner.

12. Make two mountain folds to round off the triangular flap.

13. Mountain fold the lower right edge behind.

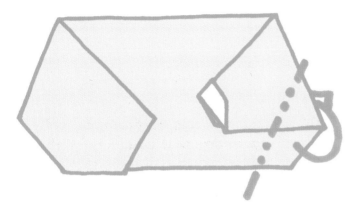

14. With a pen or pencil, draw a sleepy eye.

15. Separate the bottom edges of the paper. At the same time, push down on the top edge to create two soft curved edges, one at the front and one at the back of the top edge. The edge is flattened out, between these two curved folds.

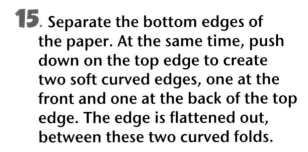

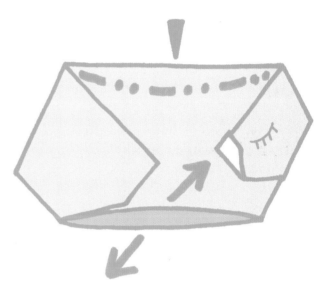

16. The Sleepy Cow complete.

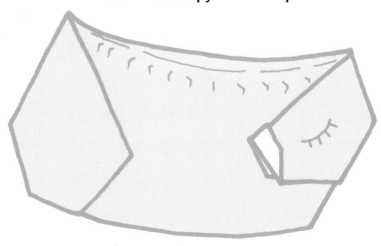

Frog

This model doesn't really look anything like a real frog, yet some-how—by the magic of origami—it is immediately identifiable as one. The most important feature is the small white triangle on each eye, which gives the model a focal point.

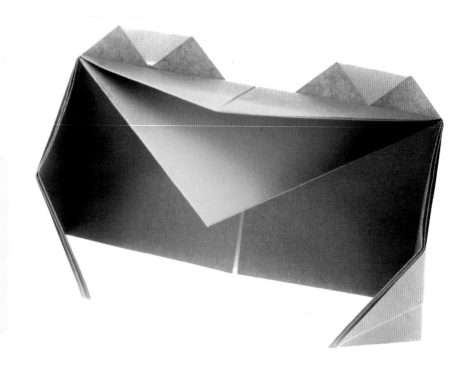

Begin with a square of paper, frog colored on one side.

1. White side up, fold in half across the middle, bringing the bottom edge up to the top edge.

2. Unfold Step 1.

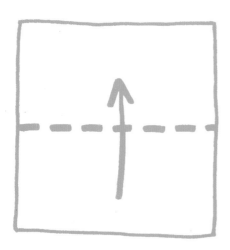

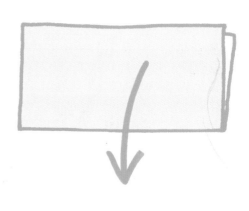

3. Using the center line as a guide, fold the four corners to the middle.

4. Fold dot to dot, bringing the horizontal edge of the triangle to lie along the folded edge. Make a neat corner on the right.

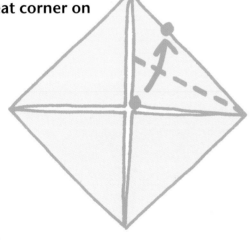

5. Repeat Step 4 on the left.

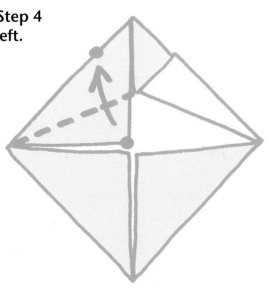

6. This is the result. Note the white paper that can now be seen. Turn the paper over.

7. Fold across the middle, bringing the bottom corner up to the top corner.

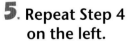

8. There are two cor- ners at the top of the paper, one behind the other. Fold them both down to the bottom edge . . .

9. . . . like this. Note how the small "eye" tri- angles are now exposed. Fold the bottom corners to the center point.

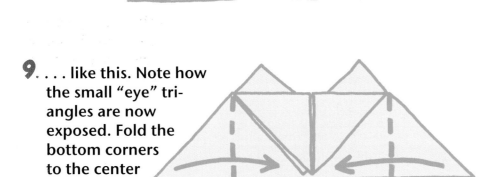

10. Unfold Step 9.

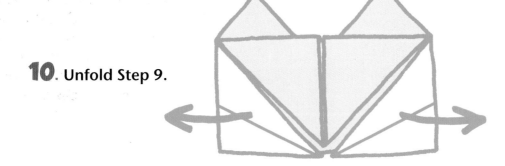

11. Fold dot to dot twice on the left and on the right, bringing the corners to the Step 9 folds.

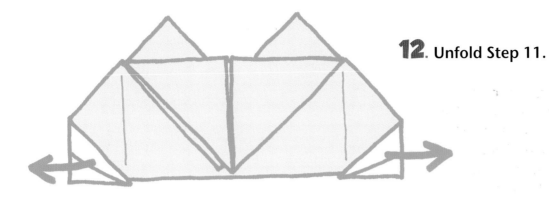

12. Unfold Step 11.

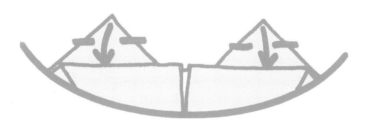

13. Fold the top corner of each small triangle down to the bottom edge.

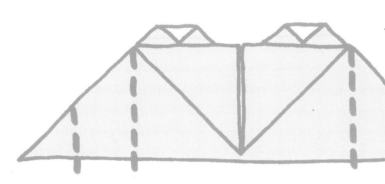

14. Recrease the folds made in steps 9 and 11. However, only fold them to 90 degrees, so that the "feet" will point towards each other below the mouth. Look at Step 15 to see the correct shape of the legs.

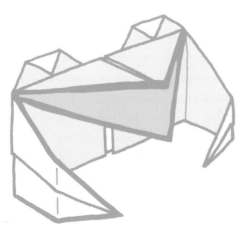

15. The Frog complete. Open the mouth and adjust the legs so that your model looks like the drawing.

Puppy

A strand of origami philosophy says that because real animals are each one individual, they should ideally be created in origami from one piece of paper. I think that's essentially true, but on the other hand, using two pieces makes many animals much easier to fold.

Begin with two squares of paper that have the same puppy color on one side. You will use one square for the head and one for the body.

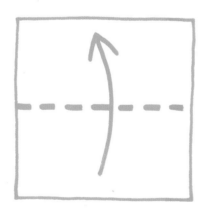

Head

1. White side up, fold in half across the middle, bringing the bottom edge up to the top edge.

2. Fold the right edge across to the left edge.

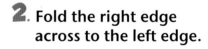

3. Unfold back to the original square.

4. On the white side of the paper, fold the corners to the center point.

5. Fold the top corner down to the bottom corner.

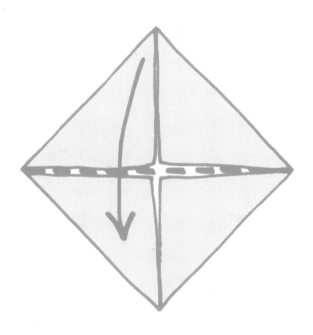

6. Fold down the top corners as shown. Note that they do not touch the bottom corner, but project outwards at the sides. Look at Step 7 to see what you are making.

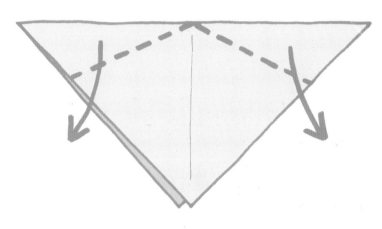

7. Round off the top of the head and the ears. Fold up the front layer at the bottom corner.

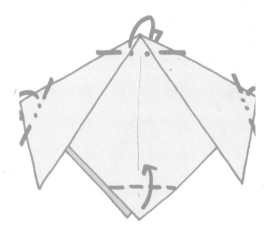

8. The Puppy Head complete.

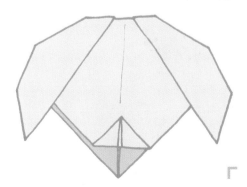

Body

1. White side up, fold in half down the middle, bringing the left corner across to the right corner. Unfold.

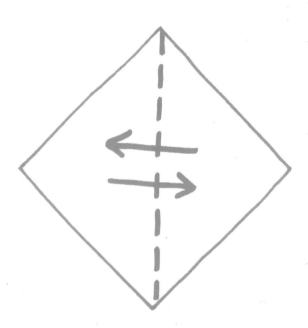

2. Fold in the top edges to lie along the center line, making a neat corner at the top of the paper.

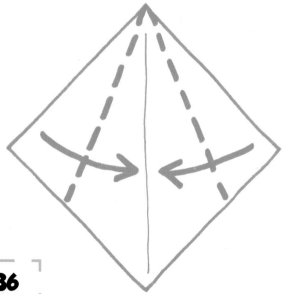

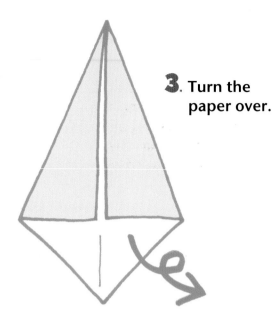

3. Turn the paper over.

4. Make a fold connecting the left and right corners, folding up the bottom corner.

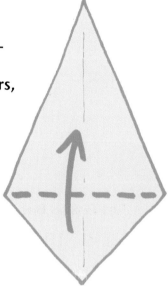

5. Fold down the top corner just a little way. Fold in the bottom corners so that each corner goes a little way beyond the center line . . .

Assembly

6. . . . like this. Note how the corners overlap along the bottom edge. Open out the corners, so that the "legs" stand forward of the body.

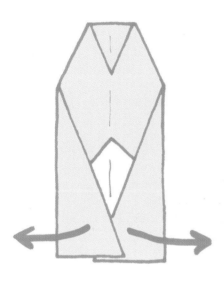

1. Lower the head onto the body, so that the top edge of the body passes up between the layers of the head. If the head sinks too low or stands too high, move the fold at the top of the body made in Body Step 5.

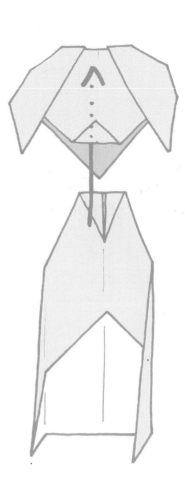

2. The Puppy complete.

7. The Puppy Body complete.

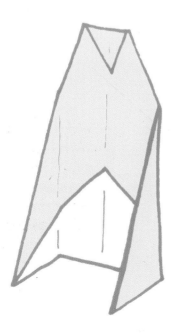

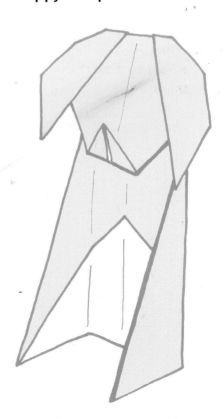

37

Butterfly

The familiar shape seen in Step 8—known as a "Waterbomb Base"—is an ideal shape from which to make butterflies. The best-known version is the all-time classic by the great Japanese master Akira Yoshizawa, and there are many others. This is my own version.

Begin with a square of paper, butterfly colored on one side.

1. White side up, fold in half across the middle, bringing the top corner down to the bottom corner.

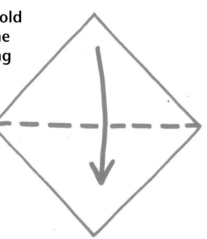

2. Fold the paper in half. Unfold.

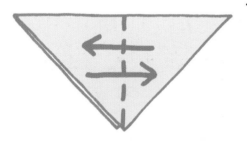

3. Fold the top right corner only down to the bottom corner . . .

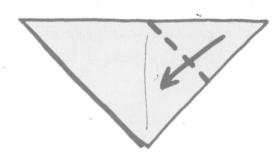

4. . . . like this. Turn the paper over.

5. Similarly, fold the new top right corner down to the bottom corner.

7. . . . like this. Continue to separate the front corners from the back corners more and more. The white pocket will first open up, and then gradually begin to close, so that the paper becomes more and more flat and triangular, until . . .

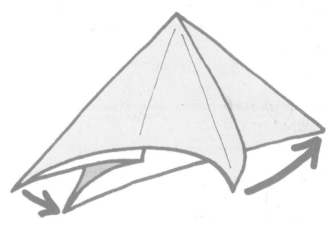

6. There are now four corners at the bottom of the paper. In the middle, between the square corners, is a large white pocket. Pull the front two corners forward and the rear two corners backward to begin to open this white pocket . . .

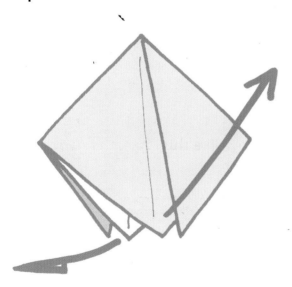

8. . . . this flat triangle is made! Strengthen all the folds. Rotate the triangle upside down, to look like Step 9.

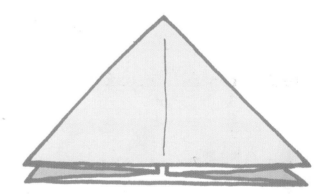

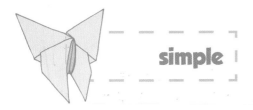

9. Fold the bottom corner up to the top edge.

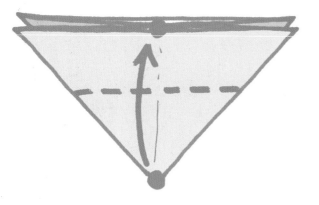

10. Step 10 shows an enlargement of the right-hand part of the paper.

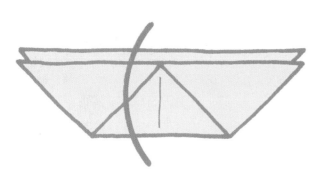

11. There are two layers at the bottom corner, one inside the other. Fold up the inside layer . . .

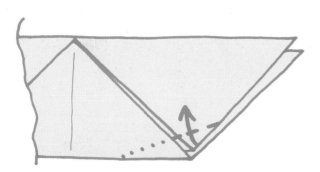

12. . . . like this, to create a skinny triangle, part of which is hidden. Repeat with the bottom left corner.

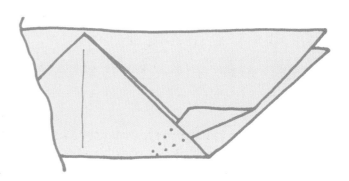

13. Fold down the top layer only to create the hind wings.

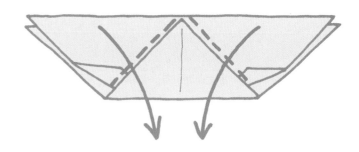

14. Turn the paper over.

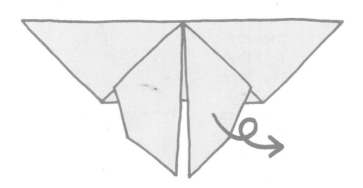

15. Fold in half.

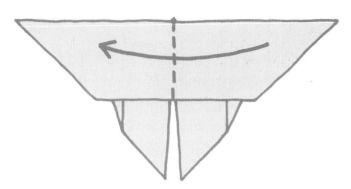

16. Make the short sloping fold as shown. Fold dot to dot, so that the front layer of wings moves a considerable distance upwards and to the right . . .

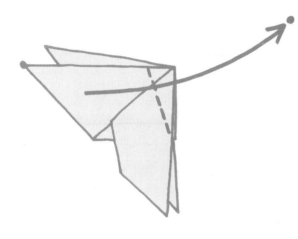

17. . . . like this. Similarly, now mountain fold the rear layer of wings behind, to lie exactly behind the front layer . . .

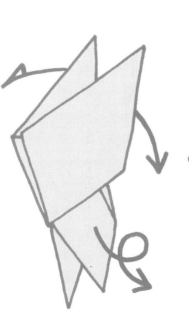

18. . . . like this. Open out the wings and turn the paper over.

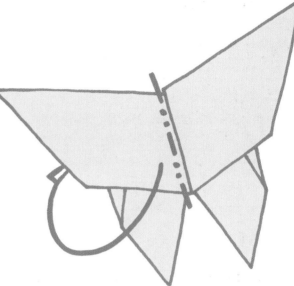

19. The Butterfly complete.

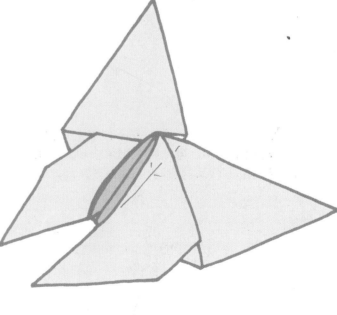

Chick

A newly hatched chick is so blobby and fluffy that the straight lines and flat planes of origami just don't seem appropriate. My solution was to create the beak at one end of the paper then to bend the remainder of the paper around a knife so that it would curve, chick-like.

Begin with a square of paper, chick colored on one side.

1. White side up, fold in half down the middle, bringing the left corner across to the right corner. Unfold.

2. Bring the bottom corner up to the top corner, but instead of folding, make a small pinch in the middle of the paper. This will locate the center point of the sheet. Unfold.

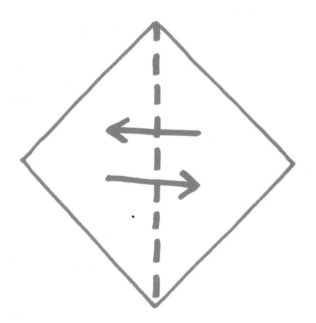

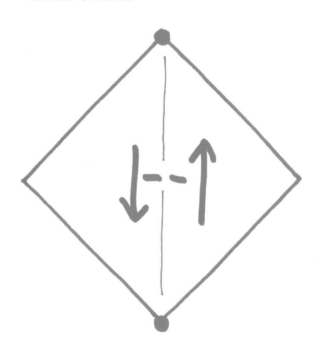

3. Fold dot to dot, folding the top corner to a point a little above the center point of the sheet.

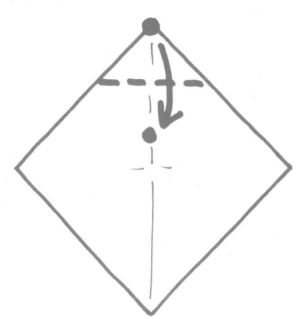

4. Fold the corner back up to the top edge.

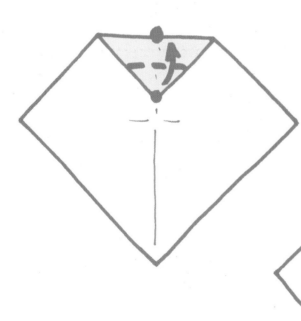

5. Fold the bottom corner up to the top edge.

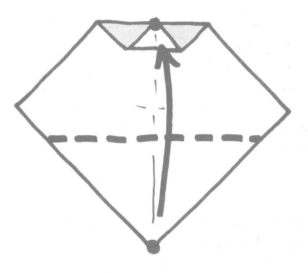

6. Fold down the front layer corner only, in line with the fold made in Step 4.

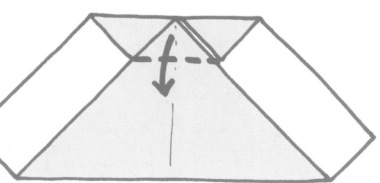

7. Step 8 shows an enlargement of the top edge.

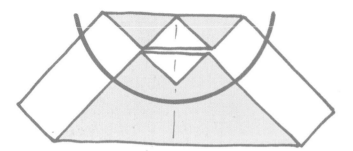

8. Fold the two white edges left of the center line to the horizontal edges. It will look like Step 3 of the Puppy Body (see page 36), but turned sideways.

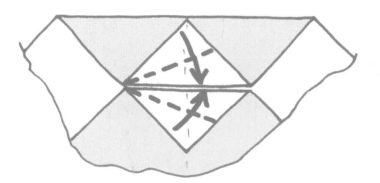

9. Mountain fold the left side of the paper behind.

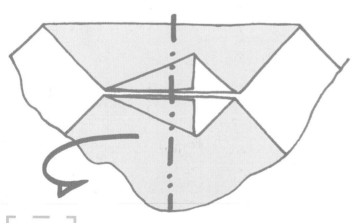

10. Pull the corners across to the left to create the beak. The new folds will look like the folds made in Step 8.

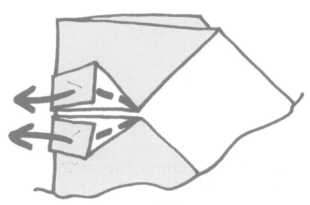

11. This is the completed beak. The front and back sides of the beak are folded the same.

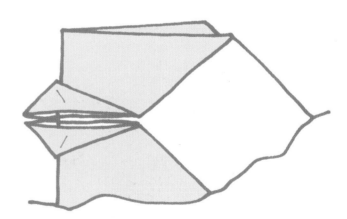

12. Make a small Inside Reverse Fold at the top of the head and a longer one below the beak (see pages 10–12 for details of how to make an Inside Reverse Fold).

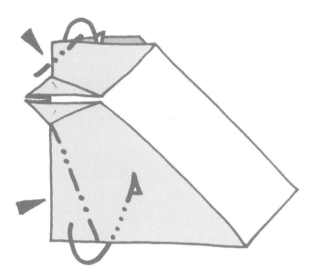

13. Use the non-cutting edge of an ordinary table knife to "quill" (curve) the paper. This is done by putting your thumb against the front of the paper, with the edge of the knife on the reverse side. Keep your thumb against the edge, then with your other hand, pull the paper forcibly through. This needs to be done with some strength. After two or three passes, the paper will be curved.

14. This is how the model will look when seen from the top: the back layer of paper remains straight, but the front side has curled.

15. Repeat the quilling with the back layer.

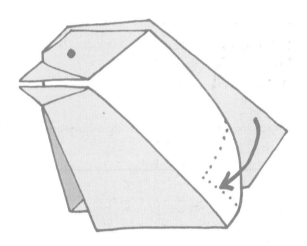

16. The Chick complete.

Dog

Like the Koala on page 16, this is another example of the extreme stylization that origami is so good at achieving. Here, the likeness of a dog is captured in just three simple shapes, one of which (the nose) is very small. A whole family of dogs can be created by changing the position of the folds in Steps 2 and 7, or by starting with a rectangle of paper instead of a square.

Begin with a square of paper, dog colored on one side.

1. White side up, fold in half down the middle, bringing the left edge across to the right edge.

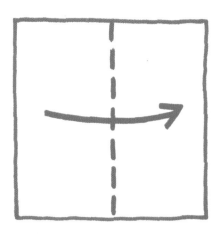

2. Valley fold as shown, so that . . .

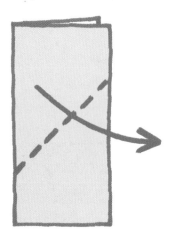

3. . . . the edges of the paper at the bottom right-hand corner create two sides of an imaginary square. Move the paper around until you have made a good approximation of a square, and only then flatten it to make a fold.

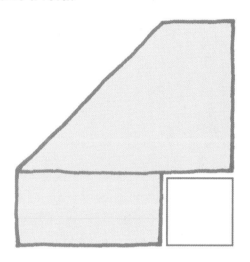

5. Inside Reverse Fold the paper, along the Step 2 fold (see pages 10–12 for details of how to make an Inside Reverse Fold).

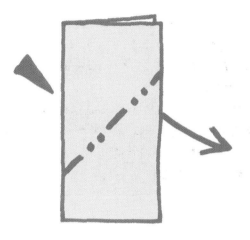

6. This step shows an enlargement of this part of the paper.

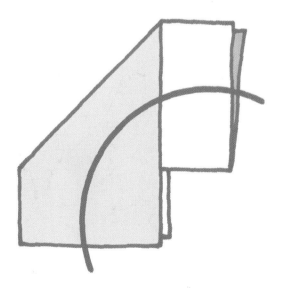

4. Unfold Step 2.

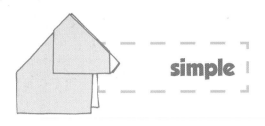

7. Inside Reverse Fold the white corner. The exact shape and size of the fold is unimportant, but about half the width of the rectangle is a good guide.

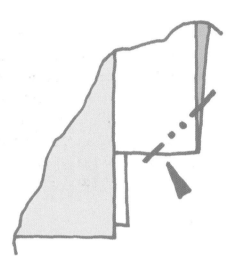

8. Fold dot to dot. Note how the fold passes exactly through the hidden internal corner created in the previous Step (shown by the dotted line).

9. Repeat Step 8 with the back layer.

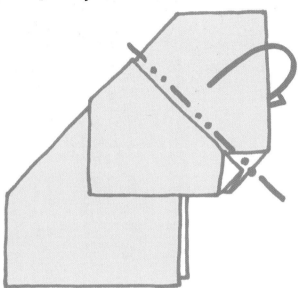

10. The Dog finished.

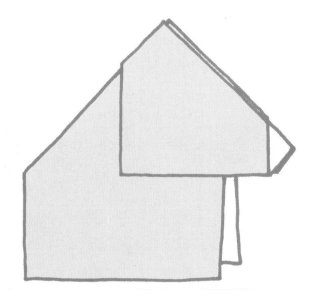

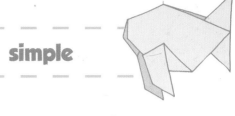

Fish

When designing an origami model, I always try to make a little folding do a lot of work. In this design, the "X" folds created in Steps 5 and 7 are located in an unusual way so that later, in Steps 10 and 15, the two parts of the "X" can be used to make two Reverse Folds that create the tail and shape the head area. I wish all my models contained "good moves" like that!

Begin with a square of paper, fish colored on one side.

1. White side up, fold in half across the middle, bringing the top corner down to the bottom corner.

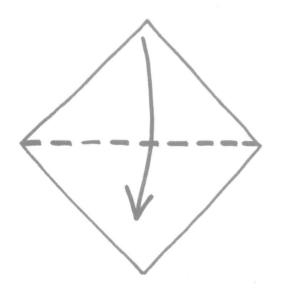

2. Fold in half down the middle. Unfold.

3. Fold the top corners to the middle of the top edge . . .

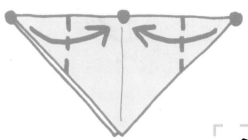

49

4. . . . like this. Turn the paper over.

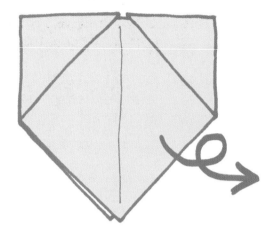

6. . . . like this. Unfold Step 5.

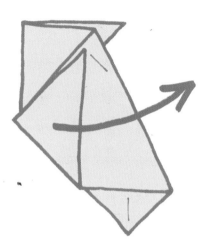

5. Fold the two dots on the right to lie on top of the two dots on the left. This will bring the vertical edge on the right to lay on top of the sloping edge at the bottom left. Note how a corner will protrude a little . . .

7. Repeat Step 5 with the vertical edge on the left . . .

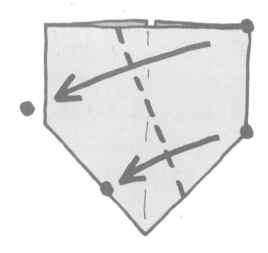

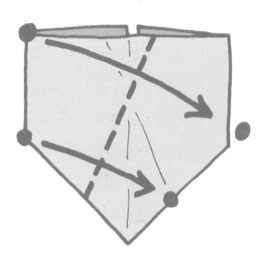

8. . . like this. Unfold Step 8.

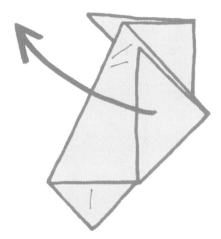

10. Make an Inside Reverse Fold (see pages 10–12 for details of how to make an Inside Reverse Fold), but using the folds made in steps 5 and 7. You do not need to make new folds.

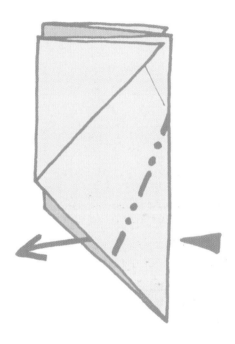

9. Fold in half.

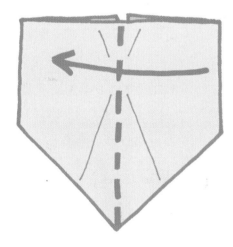

11. Fold dot to dot, folding the triangular flap in half. Repeat on the back.

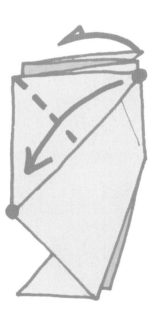

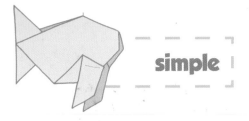

12. Step 13 shows an enlargement of the top right-hand corner.

13. Valley fold the corner, so that . . .

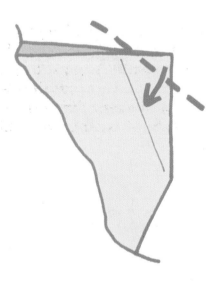

14. . . . the edge of the small triangle lies along the existing crease. Unfold.

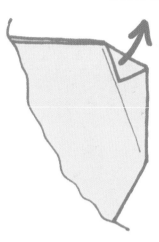

15. Make an Inside Reverse Fold, but using the folds made in steps 5 and 7. You do not need to make new folds.

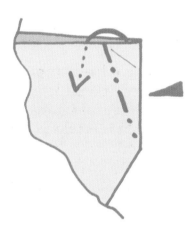

16. Lock the Reverse Fold shut using the small fold made in Step 13 . . .

17. . . . like this.

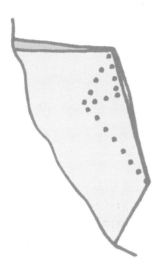

18. Mountain fold the corner inside, folding dot to dot. It may be easier to fold it first as a valley fold to help align the dots, then fold it inside as a mountain. Repeat behind.

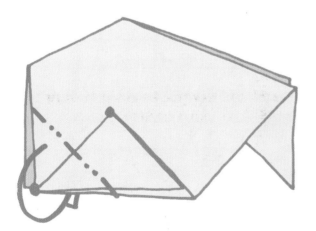

19. There are two layers inside the tail. Inside Reverse Fold the inside layer upwards to create the top half of the tail.

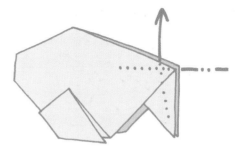

20. Swivel the fin downwards so that the dot on the right travels to the lower position. Repeat behind.

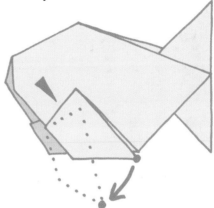

21. The Fish complete. If you want to make a fish mobile, thread a needle with cotton thread, tie a big knot in the end of the thread, put the needle inside the fish's body and pierce through the top corner. The fish will balance from this point.

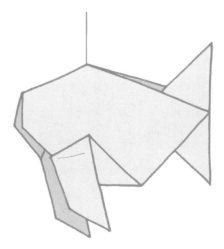

Hedgehog

There are famous and beautiful origami hedge-hogs by John Richardson, Eric Joisel and others that attempt to replicate its many spines. These technical masterpieces are extraordinary feats of folding . . . but not some-thing I could ever hope to design myself. Here then, is my much simpler spineless version, less showy, but definitely more foldable.

Begin with a square of paper, hedgehog colored on one side.

1. White side up, fold in half across the middle, bringing the bottom edge up to the top edge. Unfold.

2. Turn the paper over.

3. Fold the top left and bottom left corners to the center line, creating two large, equal-sized, white triangles . . .

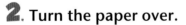

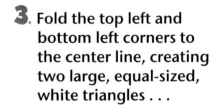

6. Fold the triangle back out to the left with a fold close to the left-hand edge of the paper . . .

4. . . . like this. Turn the paper over.

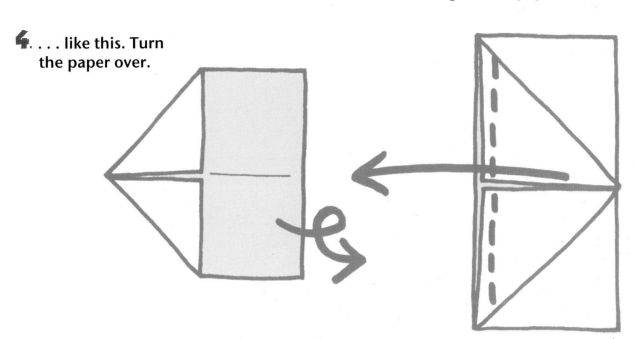

5. Fold dot to dot.

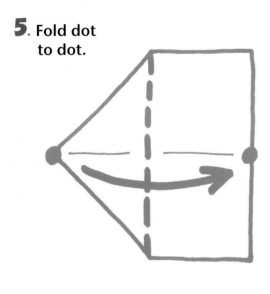

7. . . . like this. Fold the paper in half.

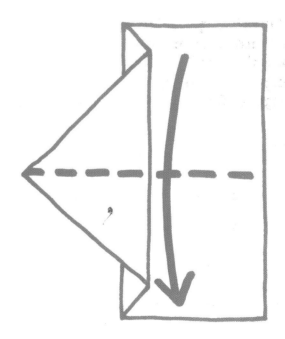

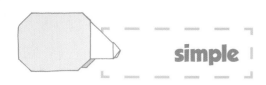

8. Hold the colored square firmly in one hand. Hold the white triangle in your other hand and swivel it forcibly downwards . . .

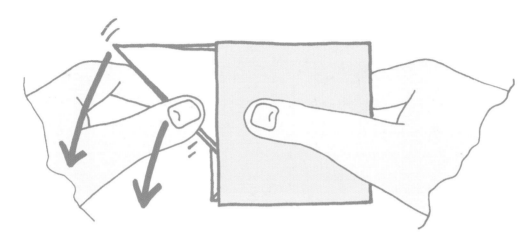

9. . . . like this, so that the bottom edge of the triangle becomes horizontal. Flatten the paper to make new folds between the layers (the new folds are here shown with dotted lines). Fold a little of the bottom edge out of sight. Repeat behind.

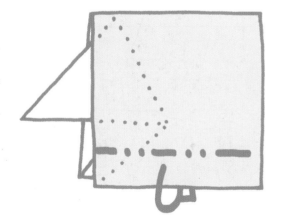

10. Fold back the tip of the nose a little.

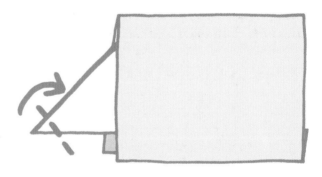

11. Step 12 shows an enlargement of the top of the head.

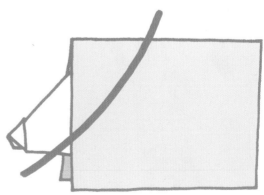

12. Make an Inside Reverse Fold (see pages 10–12 for details of how to make an Inside Reverse Fold). Unusually, tuck the triangular corner into the pocket behind the white layer . . .

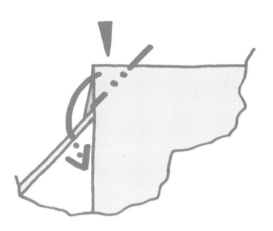

14. Inside Reverse Fold the top corner. Mountain fold the bottom corners inside. Repeat behind.

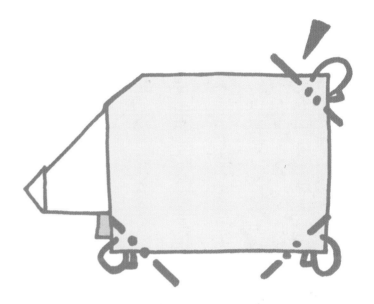

13. . . . like this (though the result is almost impossible to draw clearly!). The effect of this tuck is to lock the Reverse Fold closed into the layers of the head.

15. The Hedgehog complete.

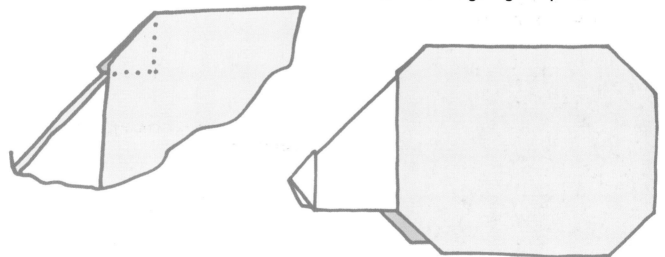

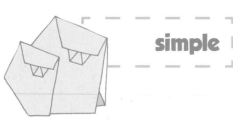

Two Monkeys

Strict origami purists would say that two animals together should be folded from two separate sheets. However, it somehow seems right to fold two monkeys together. Be careful when folding this model. The accurate placement of the folds is crucial.

Begin with a square of paper, monkey colored on one side.

1. White side up, fold in half across the middle, bringing the bottom left corner up to the top right corner. Unfold.

2. Bring one dot to the other, but instead of folding, make a small pinch in the middle of the paper. This will locate the center point of the sheet.

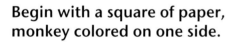

3. Fold dot to dot, again making a pinch.

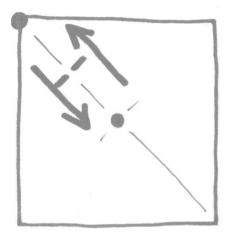

4. Fold in half along the Step 1 crease.

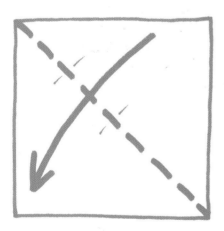

5. Fold dot to dot (the upper dot is at the pinch made in Step 3).

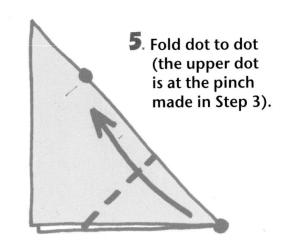

6. Fold up both layers as shown. Note that the fold is not horizontal, but slopes a little downhill at the right . . .

7. . . . like this. Unfold.

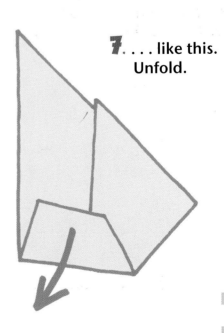

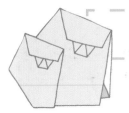

8. Inside Reverse Fold the bottom edge along the bottom edge (see pages 10–12 for details of how to make an Inside Reverse Fold).

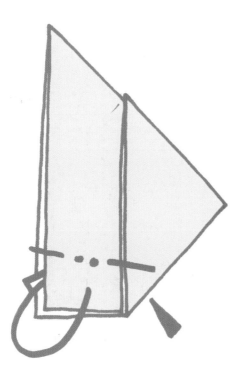

9. Fold dot to dot.

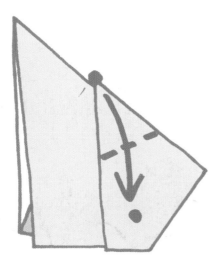

10. Again, fold dot to dot . . .

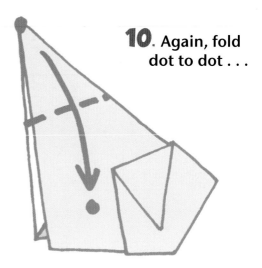

11. . . . like this. Note how the two folds made in Steps 9 and 10 create the same triangular shapes, but they are not the same size.

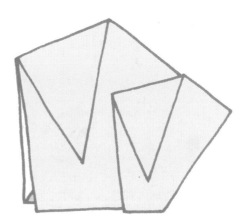

12. Make two narrow pleats.

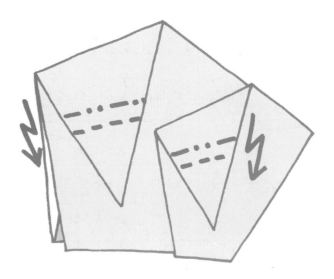

13. Fold the corners under the pleats.

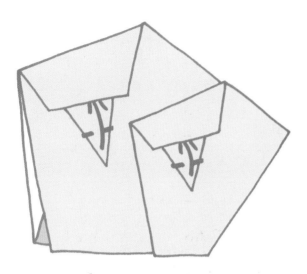

14. The two heads are now complete. If what you have folded doesn't look like the drawing, reposition the folds. Turn the paper over.

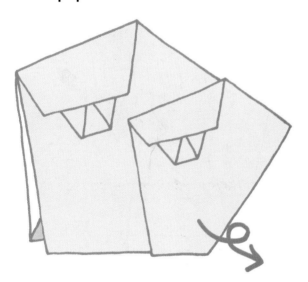

15. Make the long valley fold, squashing flat the corner at the left . . .

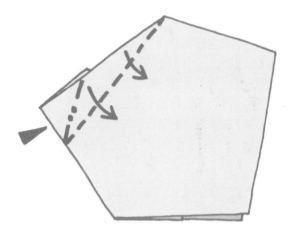

16. . . . like this. Turn the paper over.

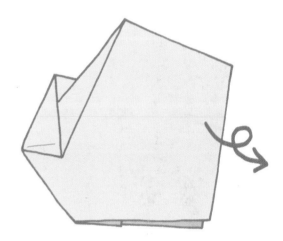

17. The Two Monkeys complete.

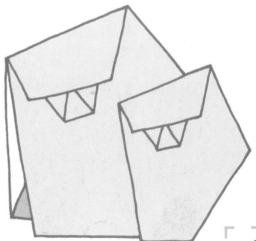

Snail

This model was created by our son, Jonathan Jackson, when he was five and a half. It's a fine model, simple and direct to fold, recognizable and original. Jonathan enjoys playing with the paper to see what he can create. To his frustration, he often creates nothing worthwhile (just like Miri and me!), but with practice and concentration, he is beginning to create excellent designs.

Begin with a square of paper, snail colored on one side.

1. White side up, fold in half across the middle, bringing the bottom corner up to the top corner.

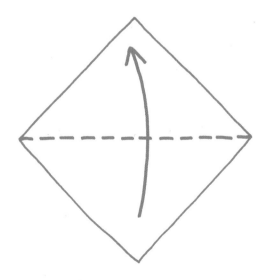

2. Fold in half, right to left.

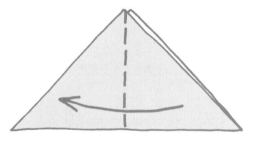

3. Open the paper completely.

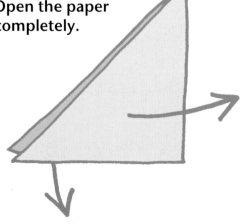

6. Fold in half down the middle. Unfold.

4. Fold in a little of the corner, as shown.

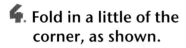

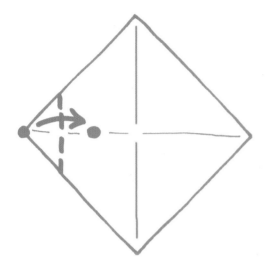

7. Turn over.

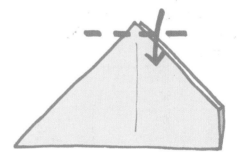

5. Check the size of the colored triangle in the drawing with the triangle you have folded. When they look the same, fold the paper in half.

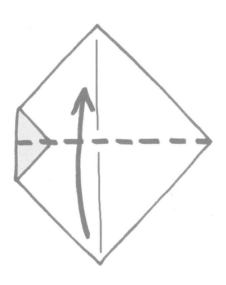

8. (Note that the fold made in Step 6 is now a mountain fold). Fold down both layers of the top corner just a little way . . .

9. . . . like this. Turn the paper over again.

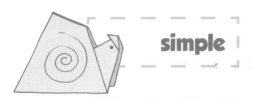

12. . . . like this. Note how the top edge of the new triangle is horizontal. Turn the paper over.

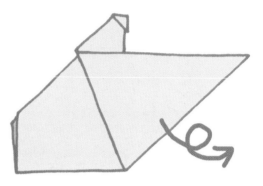

10. Fold the right-hand half of the paper across to the left.

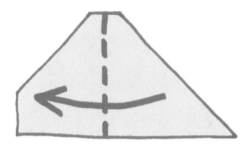

13. Fold the right-hand layer of paper across to the left, so that the new fold lies exactly on top of the old fold . . .

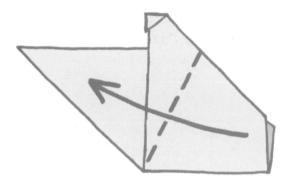

11. Fold the front layer only across to the right . . .

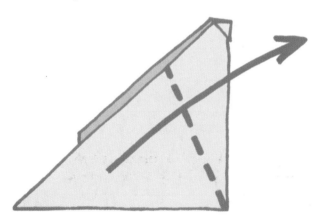

14. . . . like this. Rotate the paper to look like Step 15.

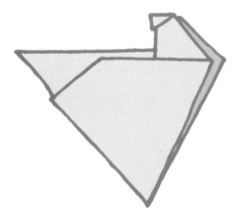

15. Tuck the top corner deep into the pocket to lock the top edge shut . . .

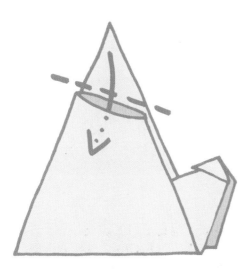

16. . . . like this (shown by the dotted lines). Step 17 shows an enlargement of the head.

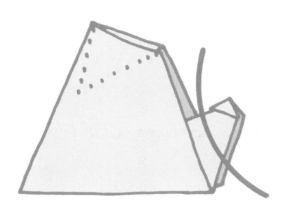

17. Pull up the small triangle . . .

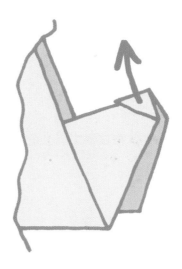

18. . . . like this.

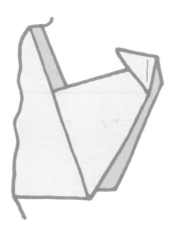

19. With a pen, add a spiral on the shell and a dot for the eye. The Snail is now complete.

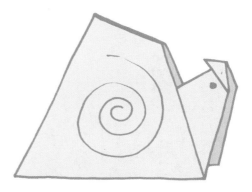

Rabbit

This model was created specifically for the book. The key step is Step 11, which locks the awkward double-fronted nose tight shut. It's an unusual move, since origami animals usually have one nose, not two. From there, completing the model is relatively straightforward.

Begin with a square of paper, rabbit colored on one side.

1. White side up, fold in half across the middle, bringing the bottom corner up to the top corner.

2. Fold in half down the middle. Unfold.

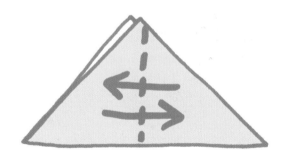

3. Fold dot to dot, aligning the bottom edge of the paper with the sloping edge. Note how the new fold begins exactly at the bottom corner of the paper. However, instead of creasing all the way across the paper, fold only between the bottom corner and the vertical center line.

4. Repeat Step 3 on the right.

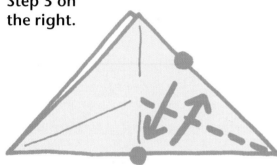

5. This is the result. Turn the paper over.

6. Fold both bottom corners to the point where the folds made in steps 3 and 4 meet each other in the middle of the paper . . .

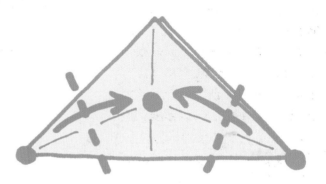

7. . . . like this. Strengthen the two folds as shown, creating mountain folds through all the layers.

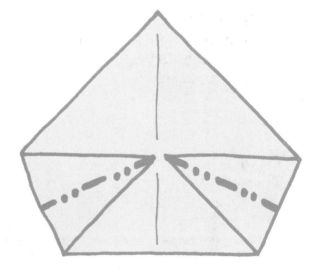

8. Collapse the paper to look like Step 9, making three mountain folds and one valley fold, as shown. The four folds need to be created simultaneously for the collapse to work.

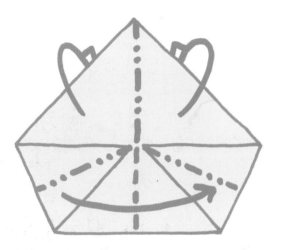

9. This is the result of the collapse made in the previous step. Pull up and squash flat the two "ears" to look like Step 10.

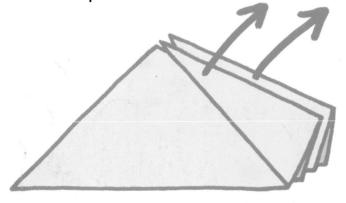

10. Note the position of the ears. Be careful not to pull them too far, or the paper will not look at all rabbit-like.

11. Open up the bottom edge of the paper. Inside is a double layer of paper, hidden from sight in Step 10. Fold both hidden layers forwards with a valley fold. Note how the fold begins exactly at the nose, locking the loose nose corner very tightly shut . . .

12. . . . like this. The nose is now a single, solid point.

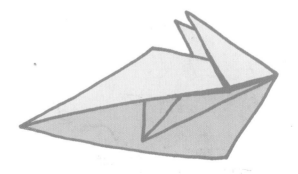

13. Inside Reverse Fold the inside layer at the tail to touch the bottom corner of the head. When complete, the result is invisible from the outside (see pages 10–12 for details of how to make an Inside Reverse Fold).

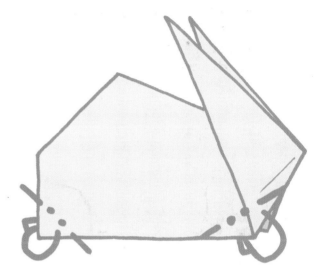

14. (Note the result of the Inside Reverse Fold made in the previous step). Make a smaller Inside Reverse Fold with the remaining layer at the tail corner. Create it by folding dot to dot, so that the tail corner comes to touch the back of the Inside Reverse Fold made in Step 13 . . .

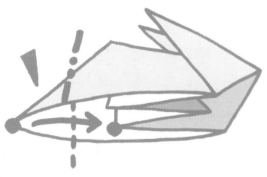

15. . . . like this. The outside of the rabbit looks very simple, but the inside layering, hidden from view, is quite complex.

16. Create mountain folds to round off the bottom corners. The placement of the right hand fold is particularly important, as it defines the shape of the head and makes the final model look very rabbit-like. Repeat both folds behind.

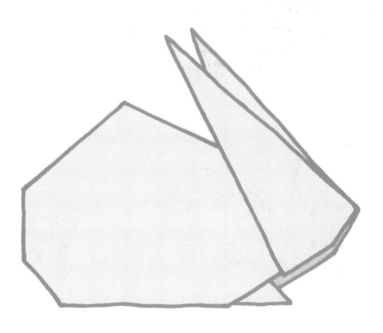

17. This is the basic Rabbit. Note how the Inside Reverse Fold made in Step 13 now peeps into view below the head.

18. Hold the top of the head very tightly.

19. Put your thumb of your other hand inside the layers of the ear and your first finger across the fold which runs down the front of the ear, squashing the fold flat . . .

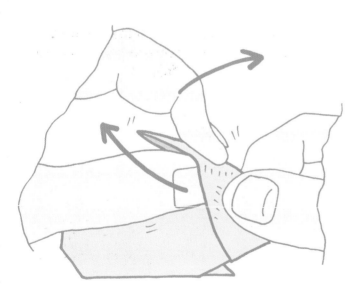

20. . . . then tweak your left hand upwards and to the right to create a kink at the bottom of the ear in the shape of an upside down "V." This kink will hold the ear open permanently . . .

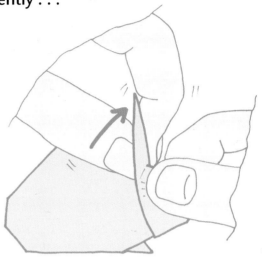

21. . . . like this. Repeat Steps 18–20 with the other ear.

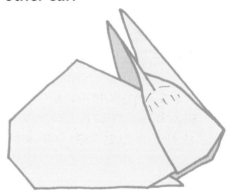

22. The Rabbit complete.

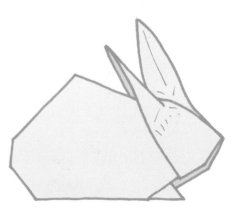

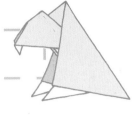

Vulture

Origami birds in flight are a good subject for beginners to try to create, since the four corners of a paper square correspond well with the head, tail and wing tips. In this standing design, the corners that might create the wing tips of a bird in flight are internalized and lowered to become the feet.

Begin with a square of paper, vulture colored on one side.

1. White side up, fold in half down the middle, bringing the left corner across to the right corner. Unfold.

2. Similarly, fold in half across the middle, bringing the bottom corner up to the top corner. Unfold.

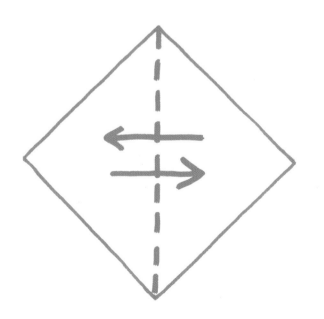

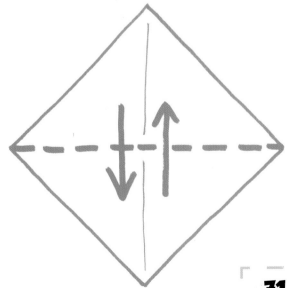

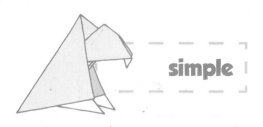

3. Turn the paper over.

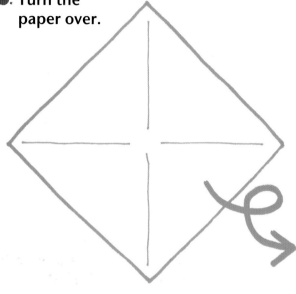

4. Fold dot to dot. Note that the lower dot is a little way below the center point of the paper.

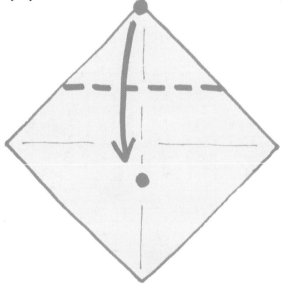

5. Again, fold dot to dot, so that the corner protrudes a little way above the top edge . . .

6. . . . like this. Check that the proportions of what you have folded are correct, then turn the paper over.

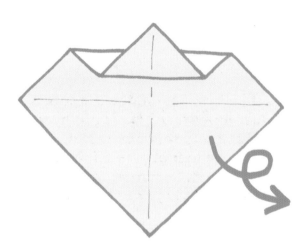

7. Fold in half.

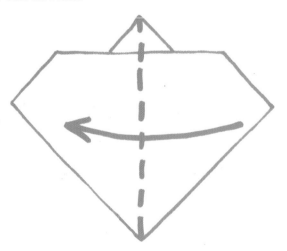

8. With your left hand, hold the bottom left edges tightly shut. Put your right thumb on the front side, as shown, and your right index finger in the corresponding place behind. Push the corner next to your thumb (and also at the back) so that the colored triangle swivels upwards just a little way . . .

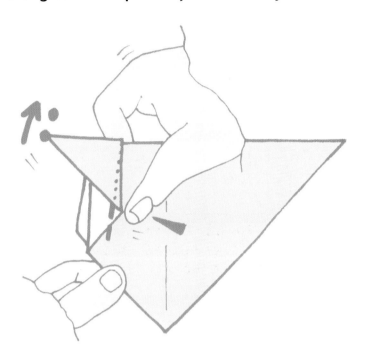

9. . . . like this. Squash the triangle flat with new folds. Now, move your right hand to hold the paper tightly shut where shown. With the thumb and first finger of your left hand, push the front and back white corners, so that the colored triangle swivels counterclockwise . . .

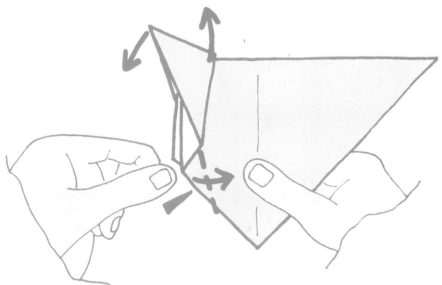

10. . . . like this. Flatten the paper with new creases. Check the shape of your paper against this drawing. If your paper looks different, remake the two swivels in steps 8 and 9.

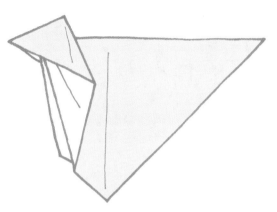

11. Fold the large triangle on the right across to the left.

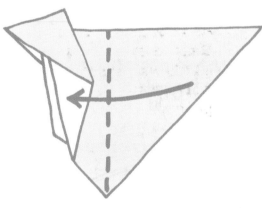

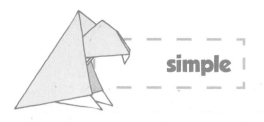

simple

15. Mountain fold the right-hand triangle behind.

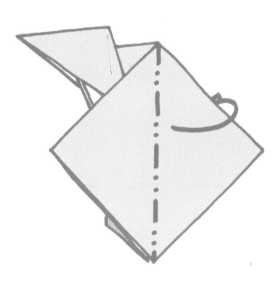

12. Stand the triangle upright. Open up the large white pocket, bringing the top corner down to the bottom, folding dot to dot . . .

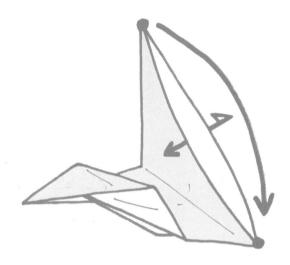

13. . . . like this. Eventually, the paper will be flat again . . .

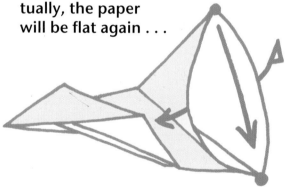

14. . . . like this. Crease it strongly.

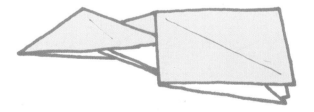

16. Open up the front layer only of the bottom edge, exposing the white paper triangle inside the tail.

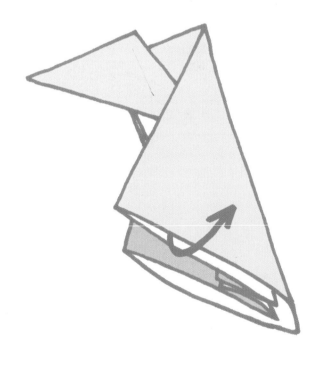

17. Fold dot to dot, pulling the double thickness white corner out into view . . .

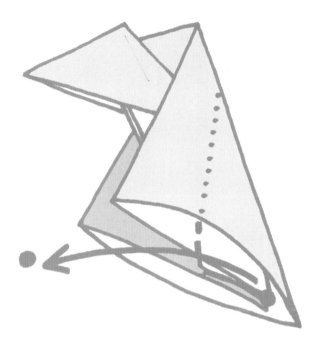

18. . . . like this. Pull it firmly forwards until it takes the position shown in the next step . . .

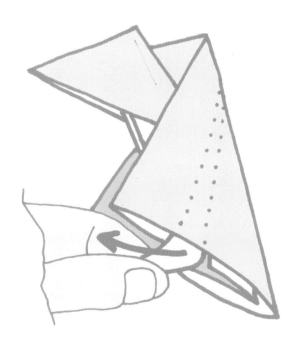

19. . . . like this. The exact placement of the valley fold can be seen in Step 17. Turn over and repeat Steps 16–18 behind.

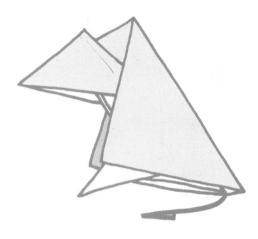

20. Inside Reverse Fold the beak (see pages 10–12 for details of how to make an Inside Reverse Fold).

21. The Vulture complete.

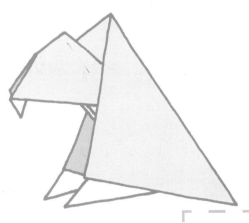

Hamster

Here, many design characteristics are shared with the Hedge-hog on page 54. In origami, not every model needs to be created from the first fold, especially when two animals—such as hedgehogs and hamsters—look quite similar. Creating a model can often lead to creating others.

Begin with a square of paper, hamster colored on one side.

1. White side up, fold in half across the middle, bringing the bottom edge up to the top edge.

2. Fold in half again.

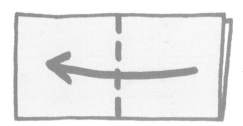

3. Open up the paper completely.

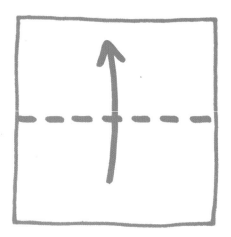

4. Turn the paper over.

5. Fold dot to dot, bringing the left edge to the center line.

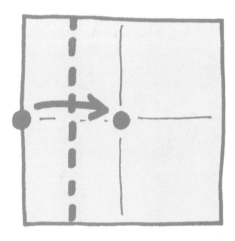

6. Turn the paper over.

7. Fold in half, bringing the top edge down to the bottom edge.

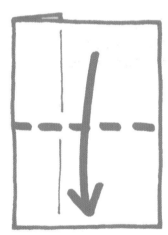

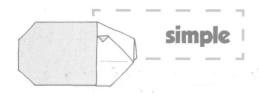
8. Create a triangle on the white paper.

9. Unfold Step 8.

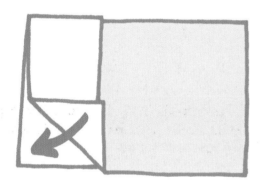

10. Inside Reverse Fold the bottom left-hand corner, using the fold created in Step 8 (see pages 10–12 for details on how to make an Inside Reverse Fold).

11. Turn the paper over.

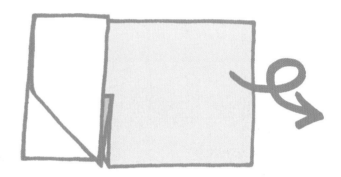

12. Repeat Steps 8–10.

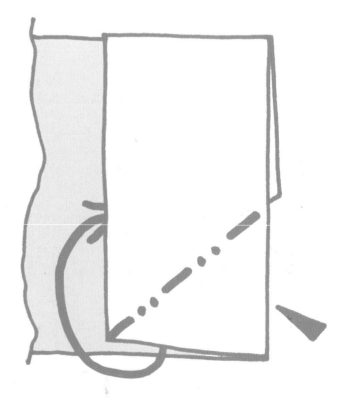

13. Unfold both Reverse Folds, returning the paper to look like Step 8.

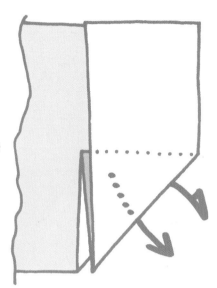

14. Fold back a very small triangle. Repeat behind.

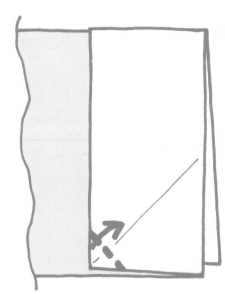

15. Refold both Reverse Folds, returning to Step 13.

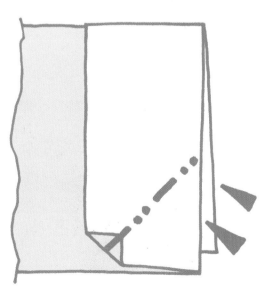

16. Note how the Reverse Folds are refolded, but they now have an additional small colored triangle. Fold up the loose flap as far as it will go. Repeat behind.

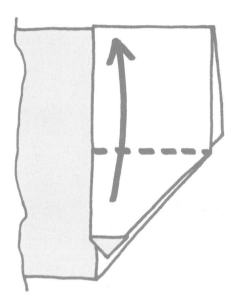

17. Fold dot to dot, bringing the top edge to lie against the white edge in front of the eye.

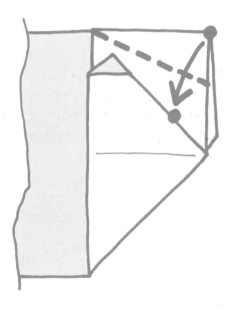

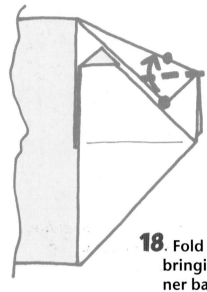

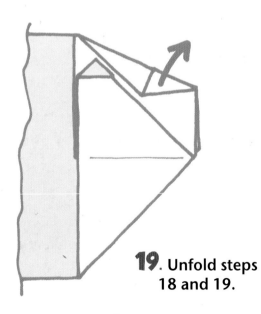

18. Fold dot to dot, bringing the corner back up to the folded edge. This creates a small white triangle.

19. Unfold steps 18 and 19.

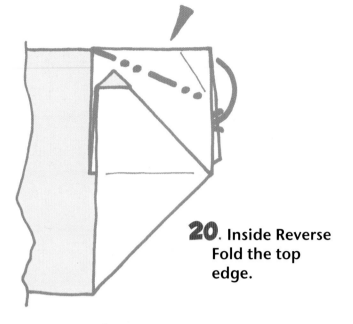

20. Inside Reverse Fold the top edge.

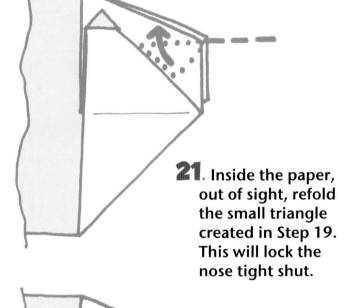

21. Inside the paper, out of sight, refold the small triangle created in Step 19. This will lock the nose tight shut.

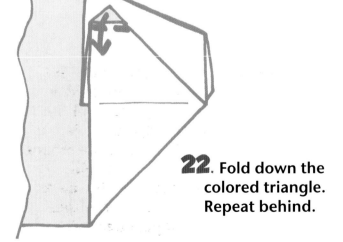

22. Fold down the colored triangle. Repeat behind.

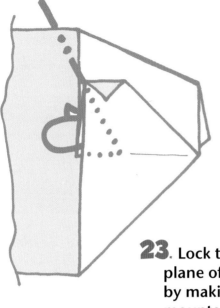

23. Lock the eye to the plane of the head by making a hidden mountain fold, as shown . . .

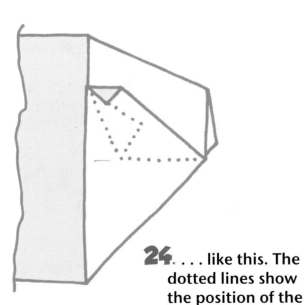

24. . . . like this. The dotted lines show the position of the hidden triangle. Note how the mountain fold begins exactly at the back corner of the eye. Repeat behind.

25. Mountain fold a little of the bottom edge inside. Repeat behind.

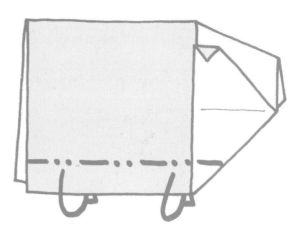

26. Inside Reverse Fold the top corner. Mountain fold the bottom corner inside. Repeat behind.

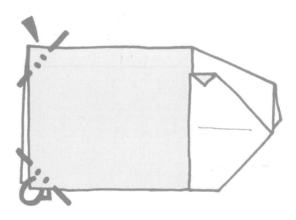

27. The Hamster complete.

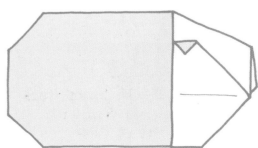

Cat

This is one of my favorite designs. All the points of the paper are used well, there are no bulked-up layers, the folding is fluent and the final model has poise and character. The head is borrowed from a design by Toshie Takahama.

Begin with a square of paper, cat colored on one side.

1. Color side up, fold in half down the middle, bringing the left corner across to the right corner. Unfold.

2. Turn over.

3. Fold the bottom left and bottom right edges to the center line . . .

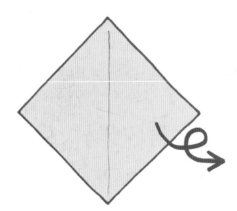

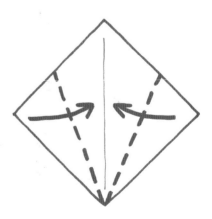

82

4. . . . like this. The paper resembles an ice cream cone. Fold dot to dot, bringing the top corner down to touch the right-hand corner. Unfold.

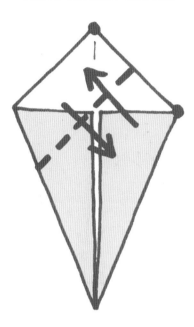

5. Repeat Step 4, this time bringing the top corner down to meet the left-hand corner. Unfold.

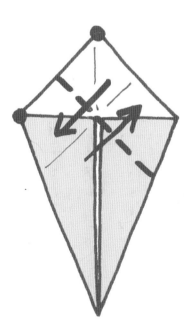

6. Make three separate valley folds and one mountain fold as shown, to collapse the paper . . .

7. . . . into this shape. The four folds must be made simultaneously. Unfold the colored triangle on the right, pulling paper out from deep inside the pocket on the left . . .

8. . . . like this. Repeat behind. Now, fold dot to dot. Notice the valley and mountain folds on the colored part of the paper. Both folds are already there, except they are currently the opposite way around! So, recrease them both correctly, as shown. Then, fold them both at the same time, together with the long valley fold on the white paper behind. This will complete the dot-to-dot maneuver . . .

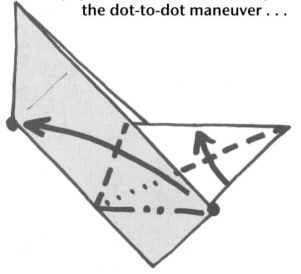

9. . . . like this. Repeat behind. Compare this step with Step 7—they have the same shape, except this step has an extra flap on the left.

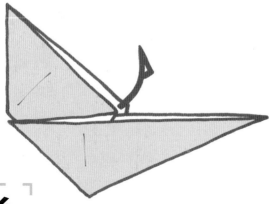

10. Valley fold, dot to dot. The corner at the bottom of the paper will become 90 degrees.

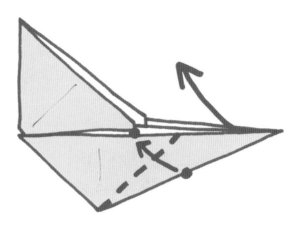

11. Stand up the thin triangle folded in Step 10. The front edge is a pocket. Open the pocket, spreading the triangle open and folding dot to dot . . .

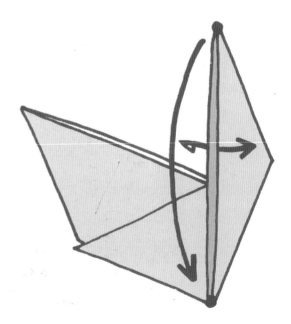

12. . . . like this. Continue to open the pocket, until . . .

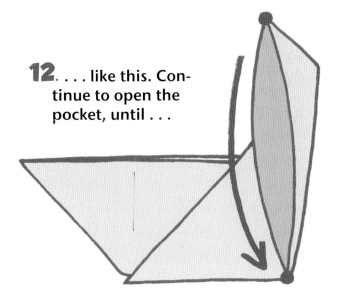

13. . . . the paper is flat. Fold dot to dot.

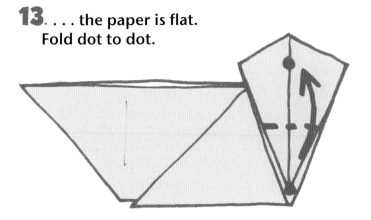

14. Unfold the Step 13 fold and refold it as a mountain fold, tucking it inside the paper.

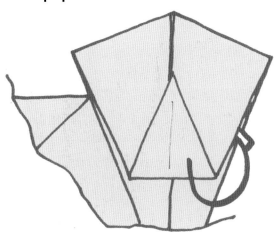

15. Make two folds. Make the left-hand fold first. It connects the top corner of the paper with the "shoulder" corner of the cat. When you have folded it, use it as a reference to then make the right-hand fold look the same . . .

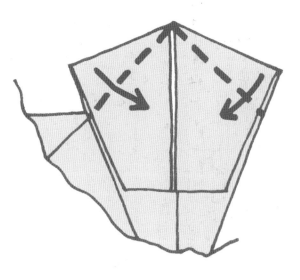

16. . . . like this. Make a horizontal mountain fold, as shown.

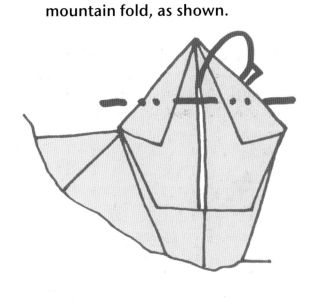

17. Make two valley folds to create the ears. Make two mountain folds to create the jaw of the cat . . .

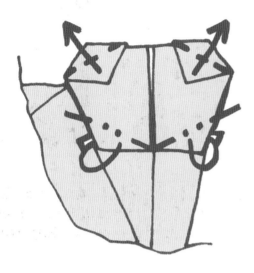

18. . . . like this. This is the correct shape of the cat's head. If the head you have made looks very different, consider refolding it.

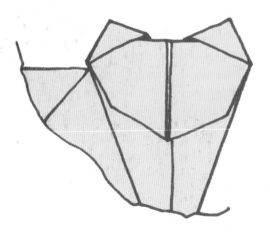

19. Fold dot to dot. Note that the right-hand dot is in empty space, beyond the bottom right corner of the paper.

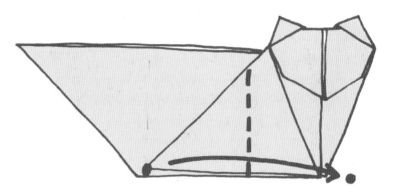

20. Mountain fold the corner inside.

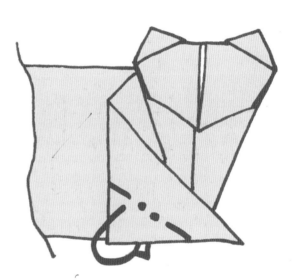

21. Fold dot to dot.

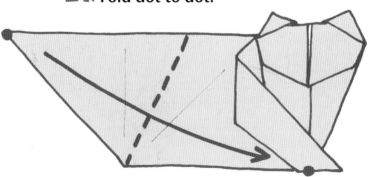

22. Round off the hindquarters with three mountain folds.

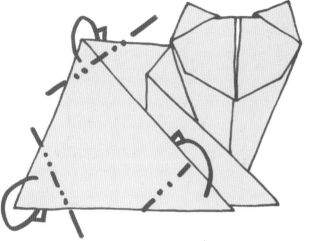

23. Turn the paper over.

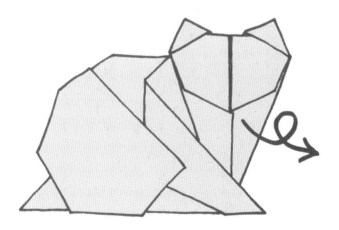

24. Fold the corner at the bottom right across to the left. Note that the top of the fold coincides exactly with the shoulder corner . . .

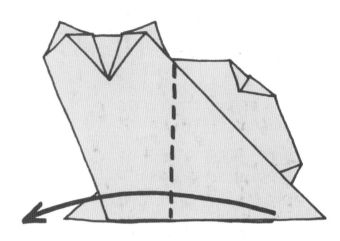

25. . . . like this. (An option with this back leg is to lock it flat to the body with a fold similar to the fold made in Step 20). Turn over.

26. The Cat complete.

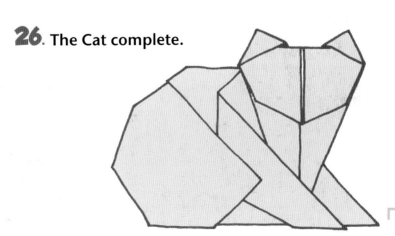

Horse

This model was created around 1978. Back then—as now—the creative fashion was to create mammals with a full set of four legs instead of just three legs (like the Horse) or even no legs (like the Dog on page 46). My contention was that four-legged animals could sometimes look over-folded, whereas simpler animals, though less "realistic," could be more pleasurable to fold. There are no designs with four legs in the book!

Begin with a square of paper, horse colored on one side.

1. White side up, fold in half down the middle, bringing the left corner across to the right corner. Unfold.

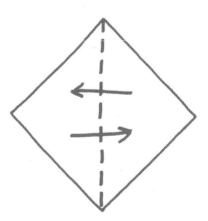

2. Fold in the top left and top right edges to lie along the center line.

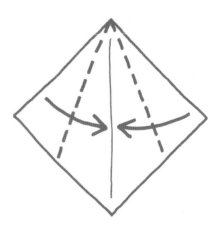

3. Fold up the white triangle.

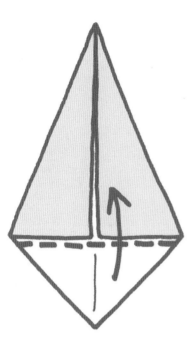

4. Unfold Step 2.

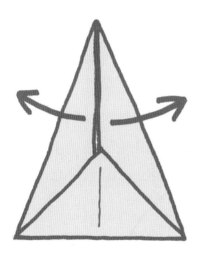

5. Refold Step 2, but now laying the left and right triangles on top of the central triangle.

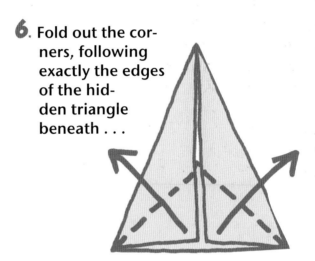

6. Fold out the corners, following exactly the edges of the hidden triangle beneath . . .

7. . . . like this. Turn the paper over.

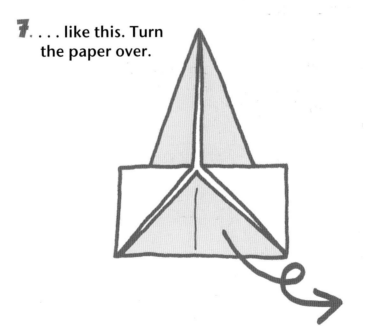

8. Make two folds, so that the left and right sections of the bottom edge lie on the center line.

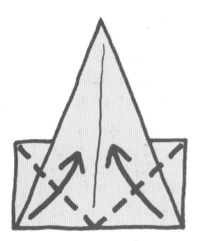

9. Fold down the top triangle.

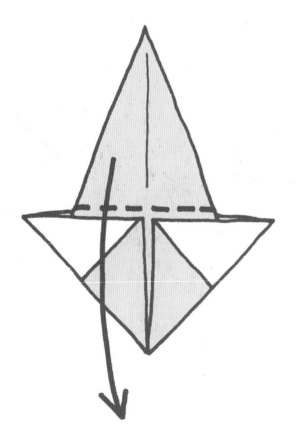

10. Fold the triangle back up, with a fold a little below the top edge.

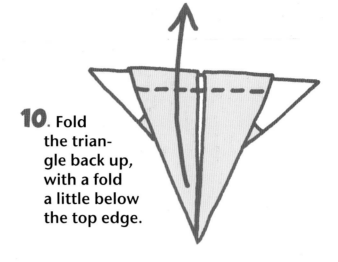

11. Turn the paper over.

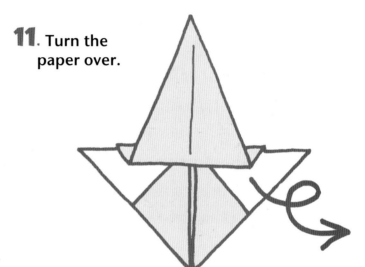

12. Step 13 shows an enlargement of the top corner.

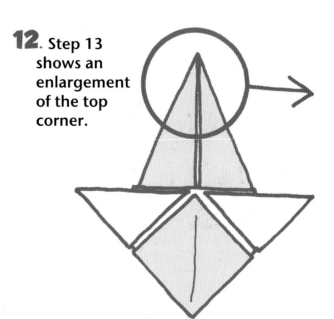

13. Fold over the tip just a tiny amount . . .

14. . . . then fold it over again . . .

15. . . . like this.

16. Make a valley fold as shown, tucking the paper under the square.

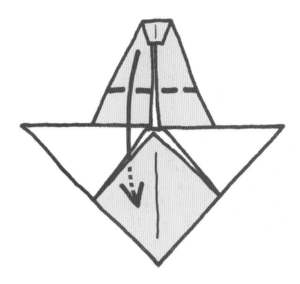

17. Fold the paper in half.

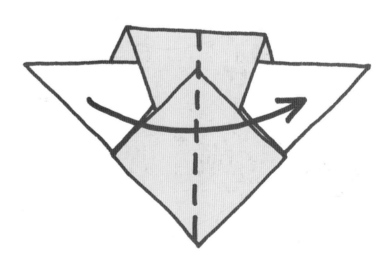

20. Pull up the tip of the square . . .

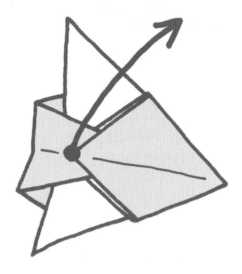

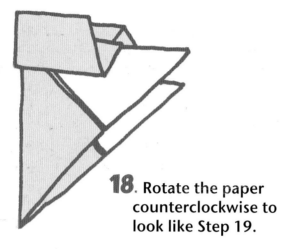

18. Rotate the paper counterclockwise to look like Step 19.

21. . . . so that it opens out into a colored triangle.

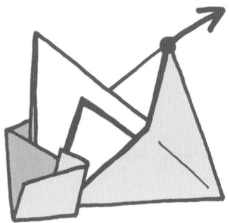

19. Spread apart the white triangles.

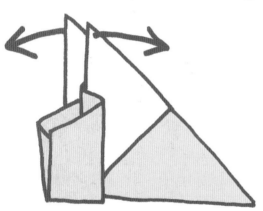

22. Lift out the head, simultaneously bringing the white triangles together . . .

23. . . . like this. The head will not be lying flat. Swivel it into the position shown in Step 24 . . .

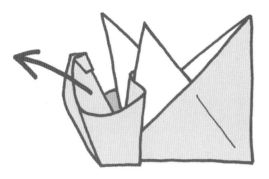

25. Fold in the corner to create the tail. Hold the horse with your left hand somewhere on the body (for clarity, the hand is not drawn) and with your right hand (as shown) at the top of the head. Swivel the head upwards as far as possible, then flatten the paper, creating a new crease across the base of the neck.

24. . . . and press it flat. Rotate the paper to the position seen in Step 25.

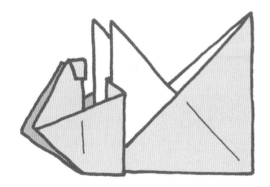

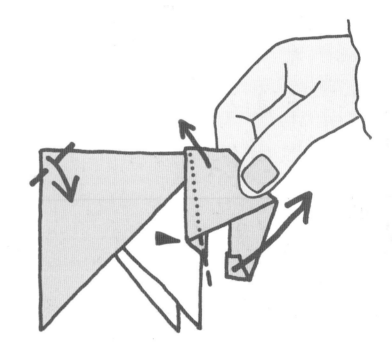

26. The Horse complete.

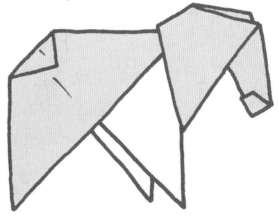

Fox

The two colors of origami paper offer many possibilities when creating models. In this model, the two colors are used to show the white areas characteristic of a fox. The design is a more complex version of a classic ultra simple fox by Mitsue Okuda.

Begin with a square of paper, fox colored on one side.

1. White side up, fold in half down the middle, bringing the left corner across to the right corner. Unfold.

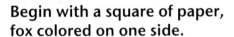
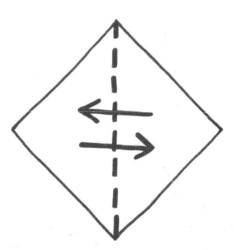

2. Bring the bottom corner up to the top corner, but instead of folding, make a small pinch in the middle of the paper. This will locate the center point of the sheet.

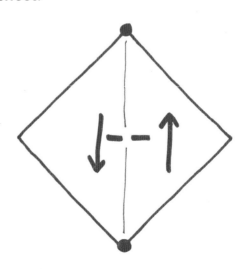

3. Fold the left and right corners to the center point.

4. Fold the corners back out to the edges.

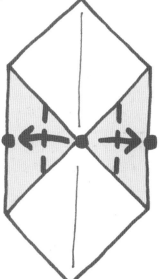

5. Turn the paper over.

6. Fold the bottom corner to the center point.

7. Fold dot to dot, so that the left edge of the white triangle is brought down to lie along the bottom edge of the triangle.

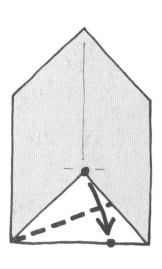

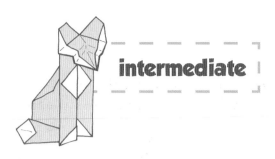

8. Fold dot to dot, folding the colored triangle in half . . .

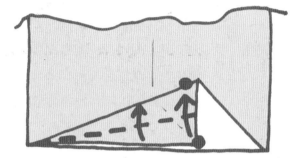

9. . . . like this. Make a vertical mountain fold, folding the left side of the paper behind the right side.

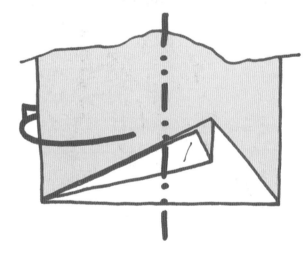

10. Put your thumb into the small white pocket . . .

11. . . . then gently swivel the top layer of the pocket over to the left . . .

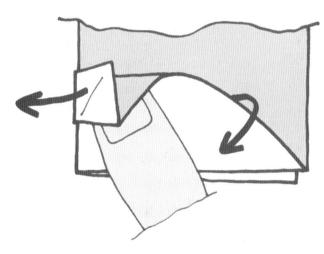

12. . . . and begin to flatten the paper with a long crease that connects the top of the pocket with the bottom right-hand corner of the paper . . .

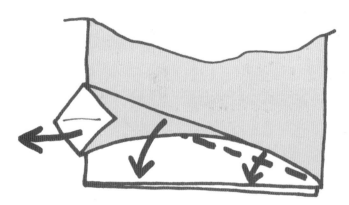

13. . . . like this. Note that the small white shape on the front is not repeated behind.

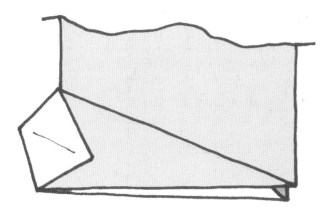

14. Make a valley fold, connecting the center point of the paper with the corner at the top right.

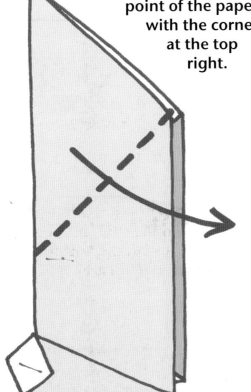

15. Fold the triangle in half, bringing the horizontal edge to the left-hand sloping edge.

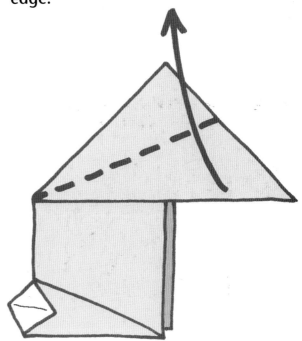

16. Unfold steps 14 and 15.

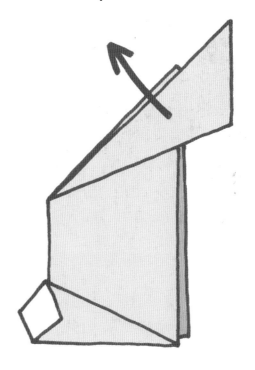

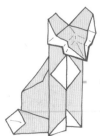

17. On the front layer only, make a mountain and valley fold as shown. On the back layer, these mountain and valley folds will already be correct. Form all four folds simultaneously, so that the folded edge (next to the drawn "push" arrow) collapses down between the front and back layers of the paper . . .

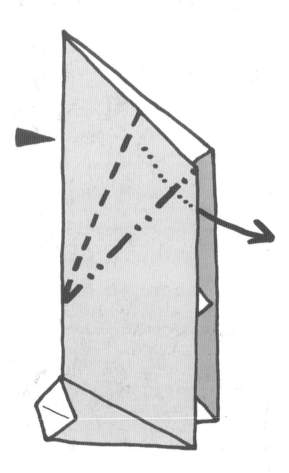

18. . . . like this. Look now at the internal point where two edges intersect, indicated by the arrow.

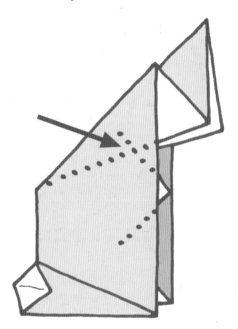

19. Peel back the front edge only, making a vertical fold that passes exactly through the internal intersection identified in the previous step . . .

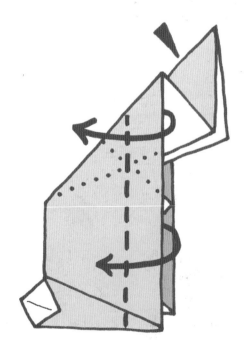

20. . . . like this. The head will not lie flat and will begin to swivel upward.

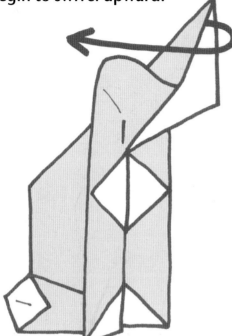

21. Fold dot to dot, flattening the head back down. However . . .

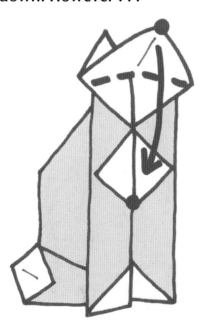

22. . . . the squash fold will end inside two white pockets at the left and right sides of the head and the paper will not want to lie quite flat. Flatten the white pockets with folds that go down to the tip of the nose . . .

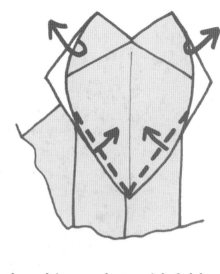

23. . . . like this. Unfold the fold made in Step 19, simultaneously raising the nose upwards and to the right . . .

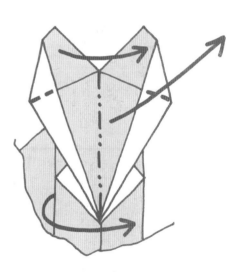

24. . . . like this. The head is now folded in half. Inside Reverse Fold the nose to the exact position shown in the next step (see pages 10–12 for details of how to make an Inside Reverse Fold).

25. Make another Inside Reverse Fold, parallel to and just below the first . . .

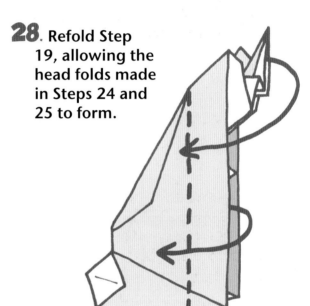

26. . . . like this. If your sequence of head folds from Step 19 has created a head that looks very different to the one drawn here, consider starting again from Step 19.

27. Turn in the back edge.

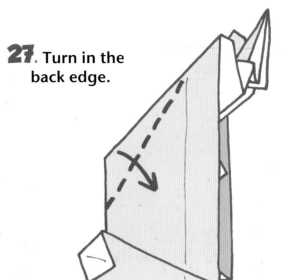

28. Refold Step 19, allowing the head folds made in Steps 24 and 25 to form.

29. The Fox complete.

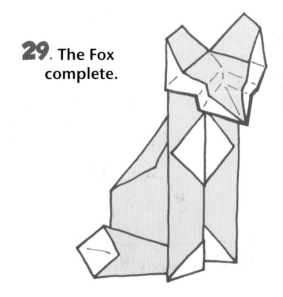

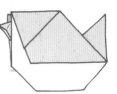
Bird

Sometimes, a model need not be a specific species, such as a Chick (page 42) or a Vulture (page 71), but can be generic. This permits the creator to be more abstract in how a folding sequence is designed. The Bird here is one of those semi-abstract, generic designs.

Begin with a square of paper, bird colored on one side.

1. Color side up, fold in half, bringing the top right corner down to the bottom left corner.

2. Inside Reverse Fold, dot to dot (see pages 10–12 for details of how to make an Inside Reverse Fold).

3. Fold dot to dot, bringing the bottom edge up to the corner.

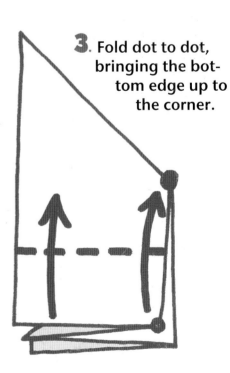

4. Unfold Step 3, but . . .

5. . . . only unfold the top layer, bringing the two upper dots down to the two lower dots . . .

6. . . . like this. The layers will spread open to create a zigzag of edges. Fold dot to dot, flattening the paper.

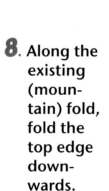

7. This is the result. Turn the paper over.

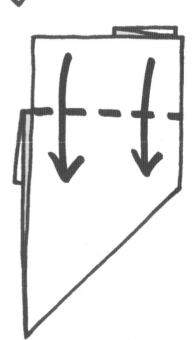

8. Along the existing (mountain) fold, fold the top edge downwards.

9. Fold dot to dot so that the square on the right enlarges to create a flat triangle . . .

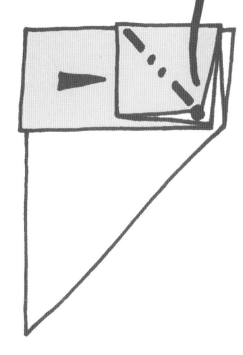

11. Make another Inside Reverse Fold.

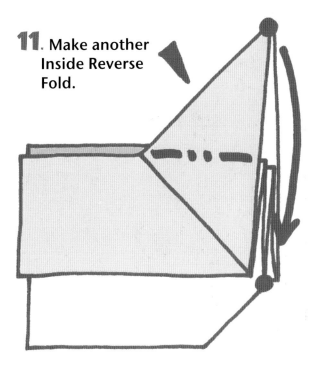

10. . . . like this. The paper is now finally symmetrical, front and back. Inside Reverse Fold, dot to dot.

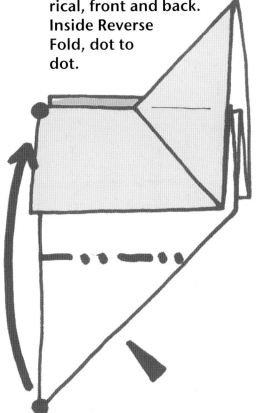

12. On the left, make a mountain fold (it might be easier to make it first as a valley, then to turn it inside). On the right, turn in a little of the vertical colored edge. Repeat both folds behind.

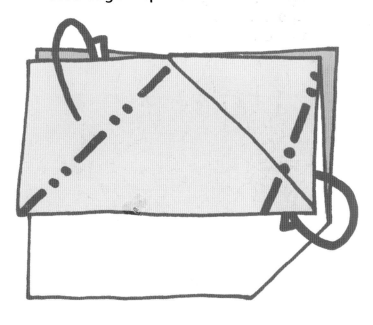

15. . . . like this. Begin to create an Inside Reverse Fold, making a central mountain fold flanked by valley folds. Notice how the three folds meet at a point below the top left-hand corner of the colored square . . .

13. Mountain fold the corner inside. Repeat behind.

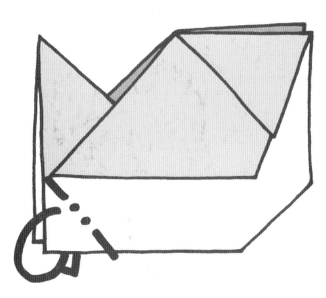

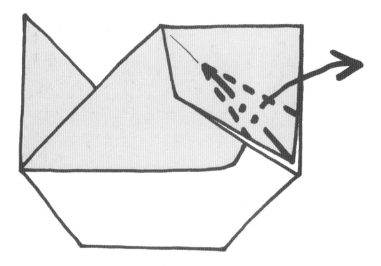

16. . . . like this. Close the square up again, flattening the Inside Reverse Fold between the layers.

14. Pull the front-layer corner forward a little way, to expose the colored square inside . . .

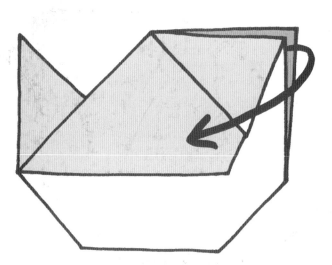

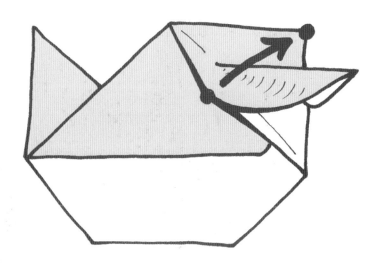

17. Note how the beak has a horizontal top edge. Step 18 shows an enlargement of the head.

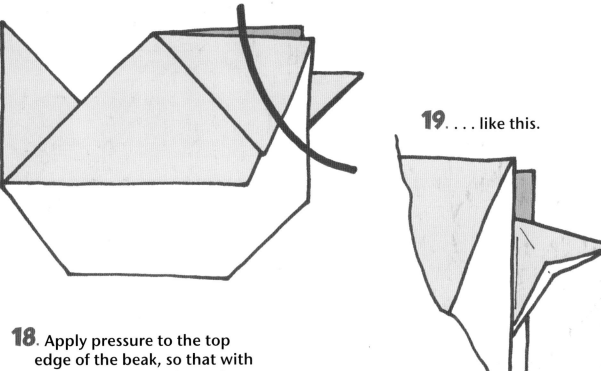

19. . . . like this.

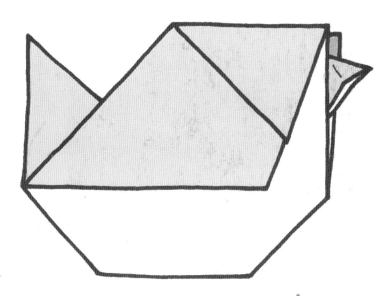

18. Apply pressure to the top edge of the beak, so that with the addition of softly made mountain and valley folds, front and back, the beak opens a little . . .

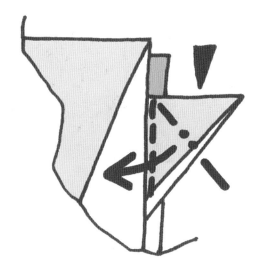

20. The Bird complete.

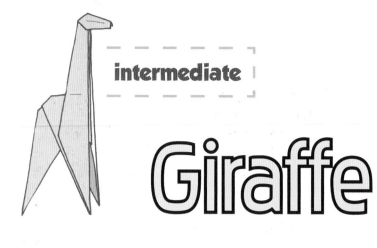

Giraffe

This design by Miri was created at the last minute and was included because we both like it so much! Interestingly for a model with a relatively large number of steps, it does not contain a Reverse Fold (see page 10) other than for the head.

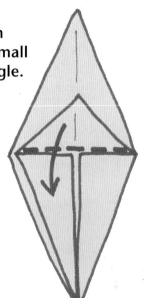

Begin with a square of paper, giraffe colored on one side.

1. Begin by folding the Dinosaur (see page 118) to Step 18. Fold in the bottom edges to the center line.

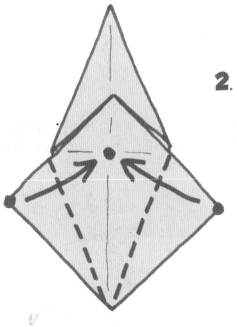

2. Fold down the small triangle.

3. Open the Step 1 folds.

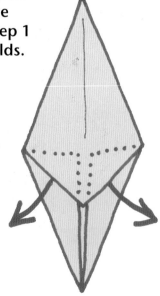

4. Lift up the small triangle so it stands upright . . .

7. In origami, this shape is known as the "Bird Base," from which many models can be created (including birds). If you learn it by heart, you will be able to make many models in many origami books. Pull apart the two corners at the top . . .

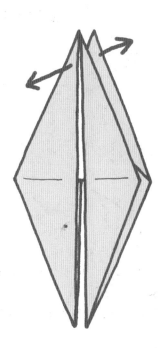

5. . . . like this. Lift up the corner with the dot, making a fold across the base of the small triangle . . .

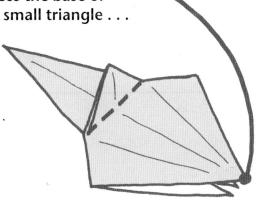

8. . . . like this. Hold the corners firmly and pull them smartly apart, so that the central pyramid flattens completely . . .

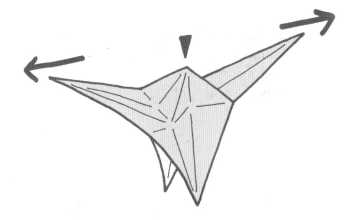

6. . . . like this. Flatten the paper, bringing the dots together. Steps 1 to 7 are a repeat of the maneuver made in steps 10–17 of the Dinosaur.

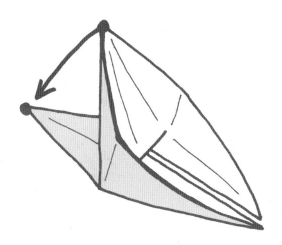

9. . . . like this. The paper is now almost flat between the corners. Make two mountain folds, as shown.

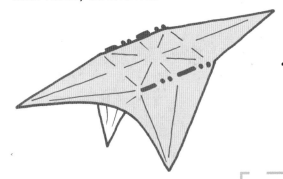

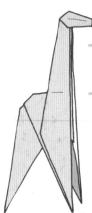

10. The central pyramid must now be inverted (that is, depressed) into the paper. At the same time, make two long mountain folds connecting the center of the paper with the top corners. Bring these corners gradually together, slowly inverting the pyramid fully into the body of the paper . . .

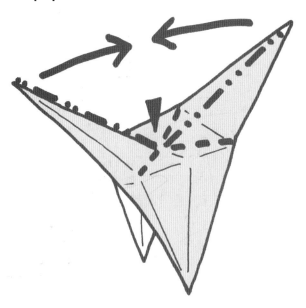

11. . . . like this. The dotted lines show the inverted pyramid structure inside the layers of the paper. Continue to flatten the paper until the corners have come together at the top . . .

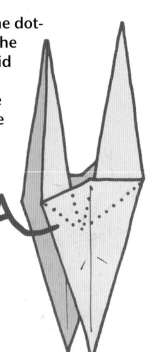

12. . . . like this. Check that the pyramid is fully and neatly inverted inside the paper. In origami, this configuration of paper is one version of the "Stretched Bird Base."

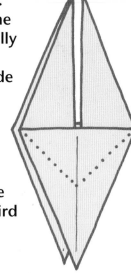

13. Fold the edge at the top left to the center line. Repeat behind.

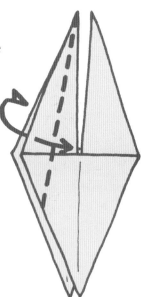

14. There are two layers on the right. Fold the front layer only across to the left . . .

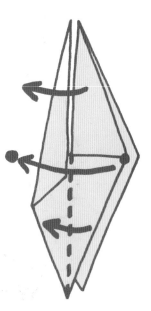

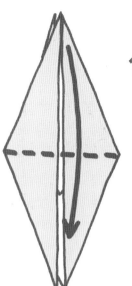

15. . . . like this. Fold the top corner down to the bottom.

16. Fold the triangle on the left, across to the right.

17. The paper is now symmetrical again. Swivel the hidden corner out into view. The dotted lines show its new position.

18. Hold the paper so that the center line is vertical. Imagine a horizontal line on which the bottom corners stand. Pull down the flap at the right until the corner lies on that imaginary line. The purpose of this alignment is to allow the finished Giraffe to stand upright, otherwise it would lean backwards!

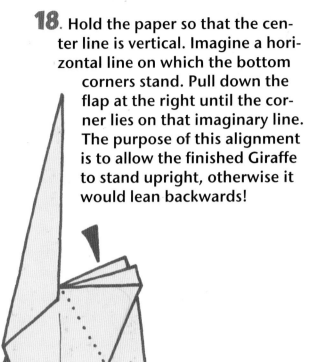

19. There are two layers on the left. Fold the front layer forwards to the right and the back layer backwards, also to the right.

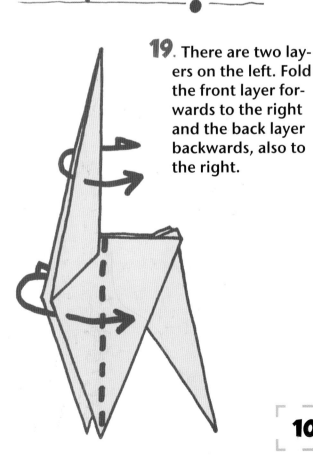

109

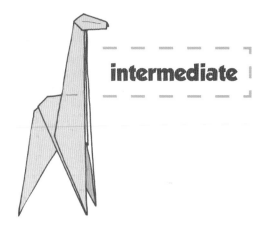

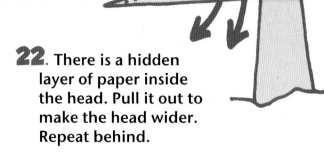

22. There is a hidden layer of paper inside the head. Pull it out to make the head wider. Repeat behind.

20. Fold in the corner a little. Repeat behind.

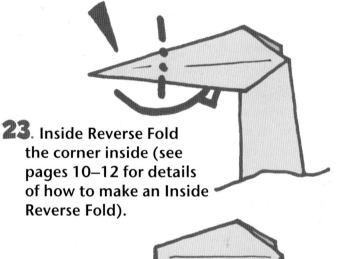

23. Inside Reverse Fold the corner inside (see pages 10–12 for details of how to make an Inside Reverse Fold).

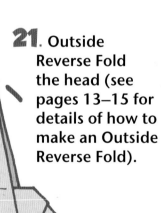

24. The head complete.

21. Outside Reverse Fold the head (see pages 13–15 for details of how to make an Outside Reverse Fold).

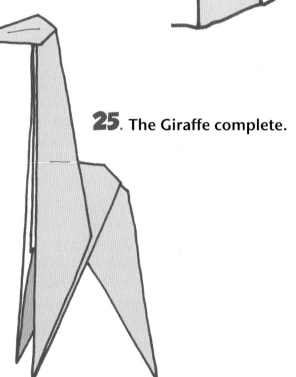

25. The Giraffe complete.

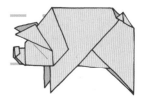

Pig

The Pig is one of a number of animal models I created that begin with the shape seen in Step 21. Others include a bear and several species of dog. The Pig is included here in preference to the others, because I like the way the head is made.

Begin with a square of paper, pig colored on one side. If you have paper that is pig colored on both sides, make a 2 x 1 rectangle and start from Step 3, treating Step 3 as single layer. It is better to make the model from a rectangle than from a square, because the final model will be only half as thick.

1. White side up, fold in half across the middle, bringing the bottom edge up to the top edge. Unfold.

2. Fold the top and bottom edges to the center line.

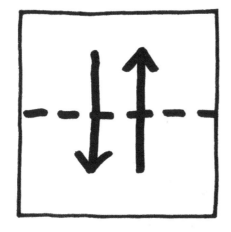

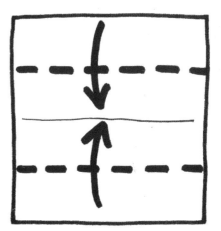

3. Fold in half, left to right. Unfold.

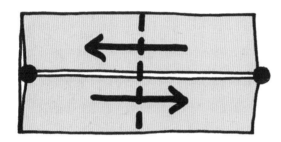

4. Turn the paper over.

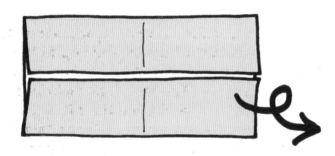

5. Fold the left edge to the center line. Unfold.

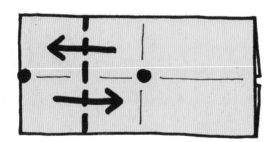

6. Fold the right edge to the fold made in Step 5. Unfold.

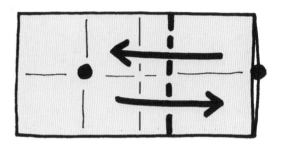

7. Turn the paper over.

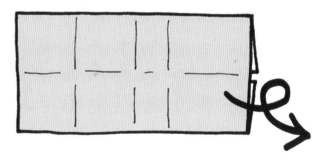

8. Make a valley-mountain pleat, using the two folds made in Steps 3 and 6.

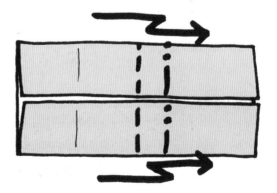

9. Create two triangles.

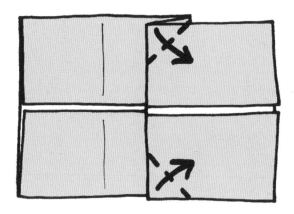

10. Fold in the top left and bottom left corners to the center line.

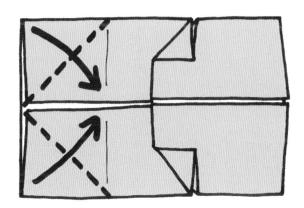

11. Fold out the corners to the position shown in the next step. Note that the folds are not parallel to the folded edge . . .

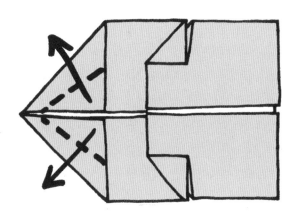

12. . . . like this. Turn the paper over.

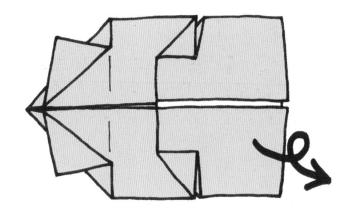

13. This is a very satisfying maneuver to do! Fold the bottom edge up to the center line to create the shape seen in Step 14. This looks like an impossible thing to do, but the triangles folded in Step 9 permit this rotation of the edge. Repeat the maneuver with the top edge.

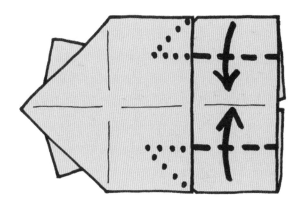

14. This is the result. If the shape is a little messy, strengthen the folds and neaten the corners.

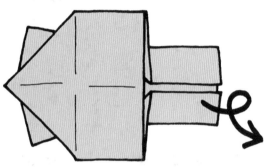

15. Fold and unfold two separate valley folds, as shown.

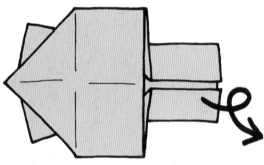

16. The paper will now become 3-D. Bring the black dots at the top and bottom across to the dot on the right, using the valley folds made in Step 15. At the same time, bring the two open circles together with a horizontal valley fold. The result of all this collapsing will look . . .

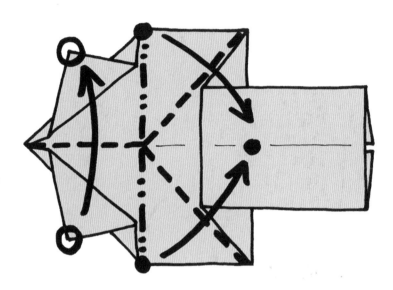

17. . . . like this. Most of the paper is lying flat, but a triangular sail stands upright in the middle. Pull out the hidden roof-shaped section of paper, marked by the dotted lines . . .

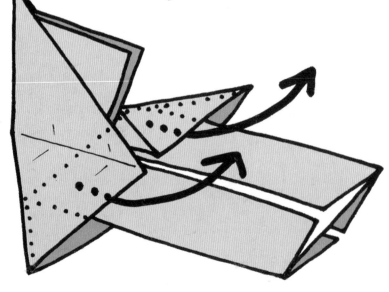

18. . . . like this. Begin to insert it back into the body of the Pig, slowly closing up the front legs as you do so . . .

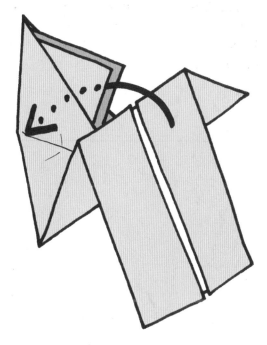

19. . . . like this . . .

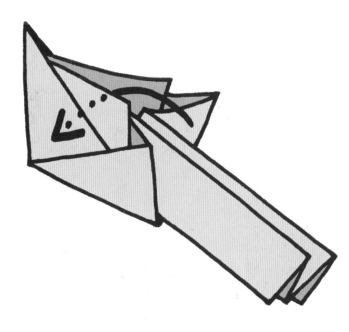

20. . . . until the paper is flat, like this. The result of the Step 18 maneuver is to prevent the Pig's forelegs from splaying open when the model is complete. No new folds have been made. Rotate the paper upside down.

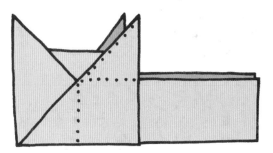

21. Step 22 shows an enlargement of the neck and head.

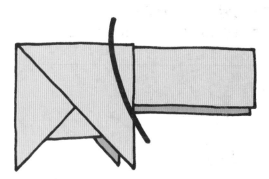

22. Inside Reverse Fold the front corner (see pages 10–12 for details of how to make an Inside Reverse Fold). Repeat behind.

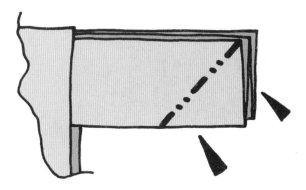

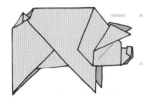

23. Fold the front and
back corners to the left.

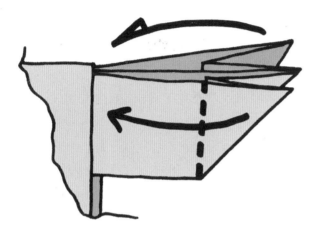

25. Inside Reverse Fold
the same corner
back into view . . .

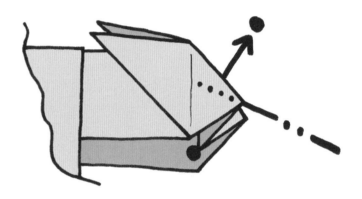

24. Inside Reverse
Fold the corner.

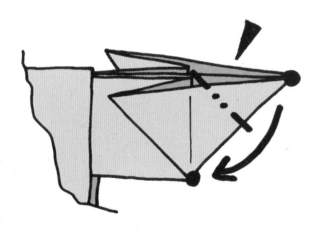

26. . . . like this. Fold
the ears forward to
the dot on the right.

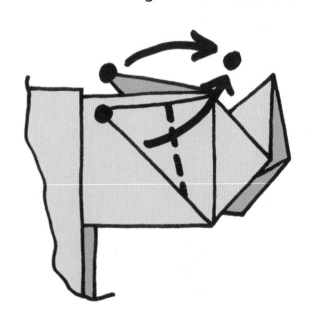

27. Fold the tip of the nose over and over.

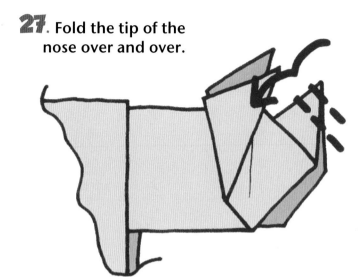

28. On the nearside layer, make a valley and mountain fold, as shown. These two folds are repeated behind, on the back layer. When the four folds are made simultaneously . . .

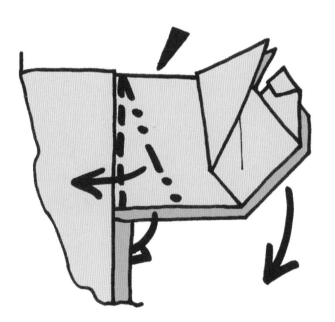

29. . . . the head is lowered, like this. Pleat the tail.

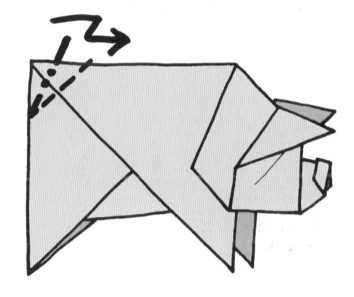

30. The Pig complete.

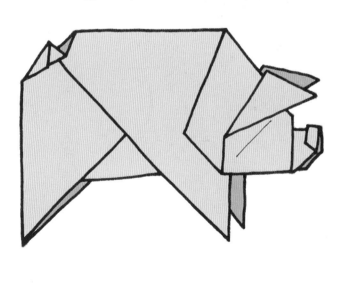

Dinosaur

Of all the models in the book, this one by Miri is probably the most challenging. It contains many steps and also many Inside and Outside Reverse Folds (see pages 10–15) that need to be made with precision. It is also the only model to contain cuts, to create the forelegs. There are ways to create the legs without cuts, but cutting them free is the simplest and most elegant way to create them.

Begin with a square of paper, dinosaur colored on one side.

1. White side up, fold the paper in half, bringing the top edge down to the bottom edge.

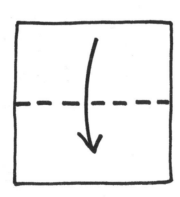

2. Fold in half, bringing the left edge across to the right.

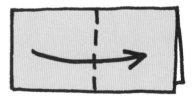

3. Unfold Step 2.

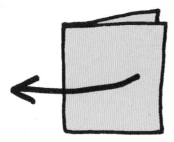

6. In a similar way to Step 4, fold down the top right-hand corner.

4. Fold dot to dot, bringing the top right-hand corner down to the middle of the bottom edge . . .

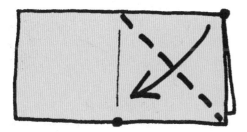

7. Use a finger to open the large white pocket in the middle of the layers . . .

5. . . . like this. Turn the paper over.

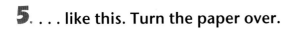

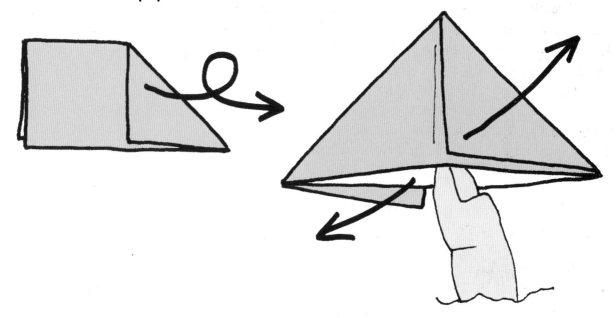

8. . . . like this. Continue to open the triangular white pocket more and more until it begins to close. Apply pressure on the folded edges on the left and right, allowing the two dotted corners to come together . . .

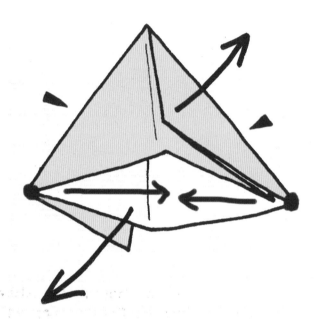

9. . . . like this, in the shape of a square. Flatten the paper.

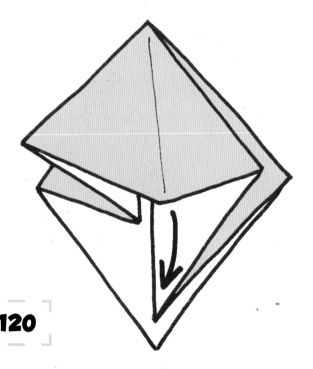

10. This is the result. Note that the center of the original square of paper is now at the top corner and the bottom corner is messy and open. Fold in the bottom left and bottom right edges of the square to the center line . . .

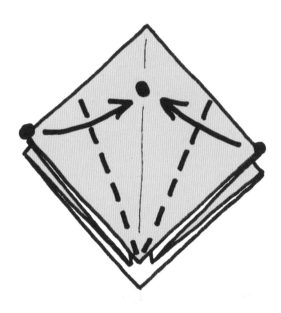

11. . . . like this. Fold down the top triangle.

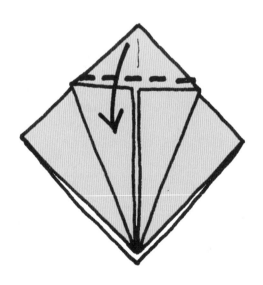

12. Open the
Step 10 folds.

13. Stand up the triangle
at 90 degrees . . .

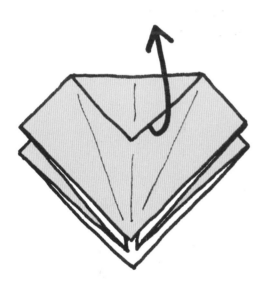

14. . . . like this. Pick up the single thickness corner and swing it up and over towards the left, using the valley fold across the base of the upright triangle as a pivot . . .

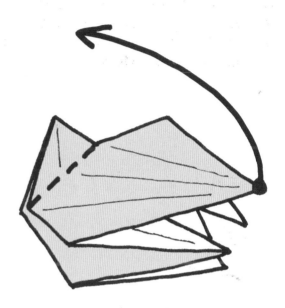

15. . . . like this. Note how a lot of white paper can be seen. Gently collapse the paper flat, slowly closing the white pocket and bringing the top corner downwards.

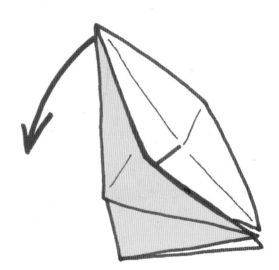

16. Note how when making Step 15, it helps to keep the small triangle held against the back of the pocket.

17. Eventually, the white pocket will close up and the paper will once again be flat. The top corner should close neatly, but if it's a little messy, move the folds around a little. Turn the paper over.

18. Repeat Step 10, folding the bottom edges to the center line. Unfold.

19. Repeat Step 11, folding down the central triangle. Unfold.

20. Apply pressure to the edge on the left, so that the front square opens and the bottom corner moves a long way upwards and to the right, to the dot . . .

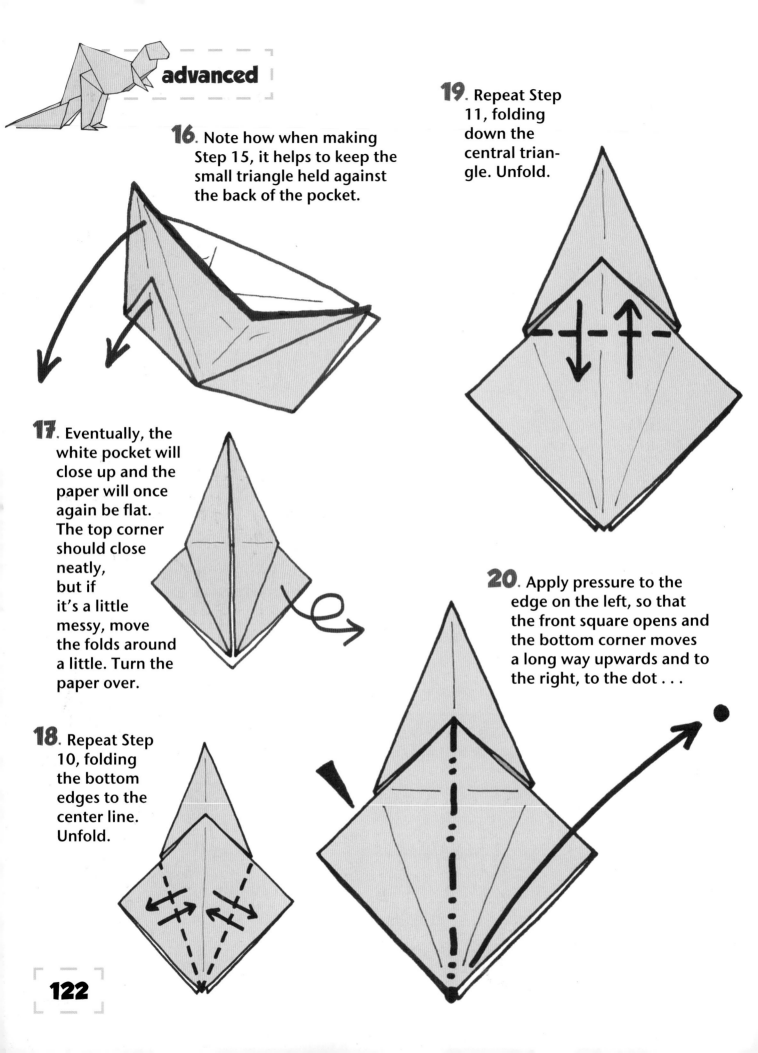

21. . . . like this. Turn the paper over.

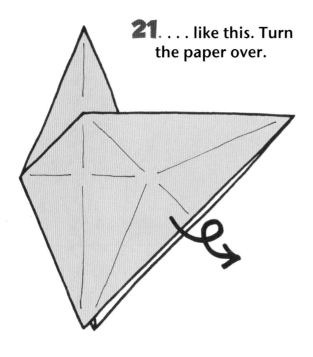

24. The paper is now symmetrical, front and back. Fold up the front corner as far as it will go.

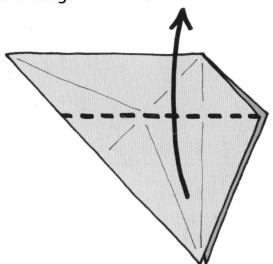

22. Fold the top corner down to the bottom corner.

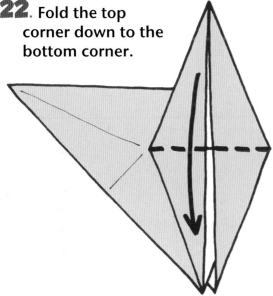

23. Fold the loose flap over to the right.

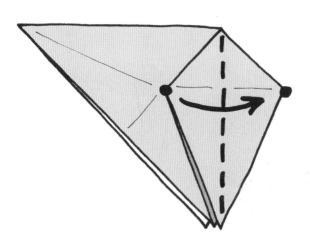

25. Swivel the colored triangle on the right across to the left. At the same time, collapse the white triangle at the top left, bringing the upper dot down to the lower dot. Quite a lot of the paper changes position in this step, but the result . . .

123

28. Fold up the bottom corner. This is a repeat of Step 24. Then, continue with the collapsing sequence made in Steps 25 and 26.

26. . . . will look like this. Note the complex layering of the paper towards the top left. Inside Reverse Fold the triangle inside . . .

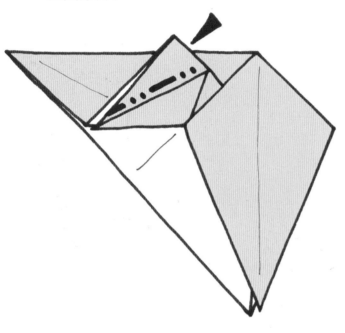

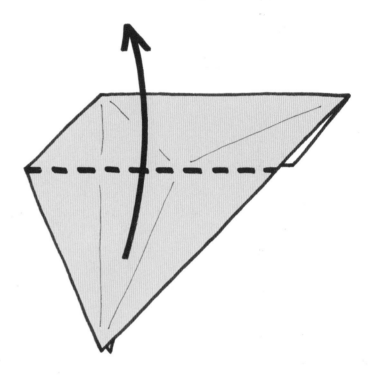

27. . . . like this, to create a long, narrow free point. Turn the paper over.

29. The paper is now symmetrical, front and back. Outside Reverse Fold the bottom corner out to the left. Note the precise placement of the fold.

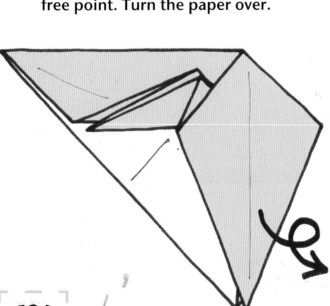

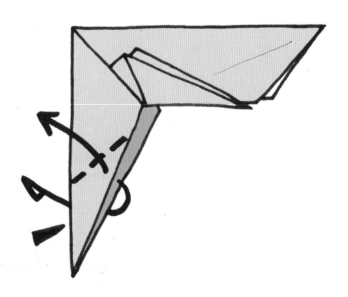

30. Similarly, Outside Reverse Fold the central layers of paper at the right. Again, look carefully to note the exact placement of the fold.

31. Narrow the paper by folding in half along the existing crease. Repeat behind.

33. Outside Reverse Fold the head.

32. Step 33 shows an enlargement of the head.

34. Pull out the hidden single layer of paper inside the head. Repeat behind.

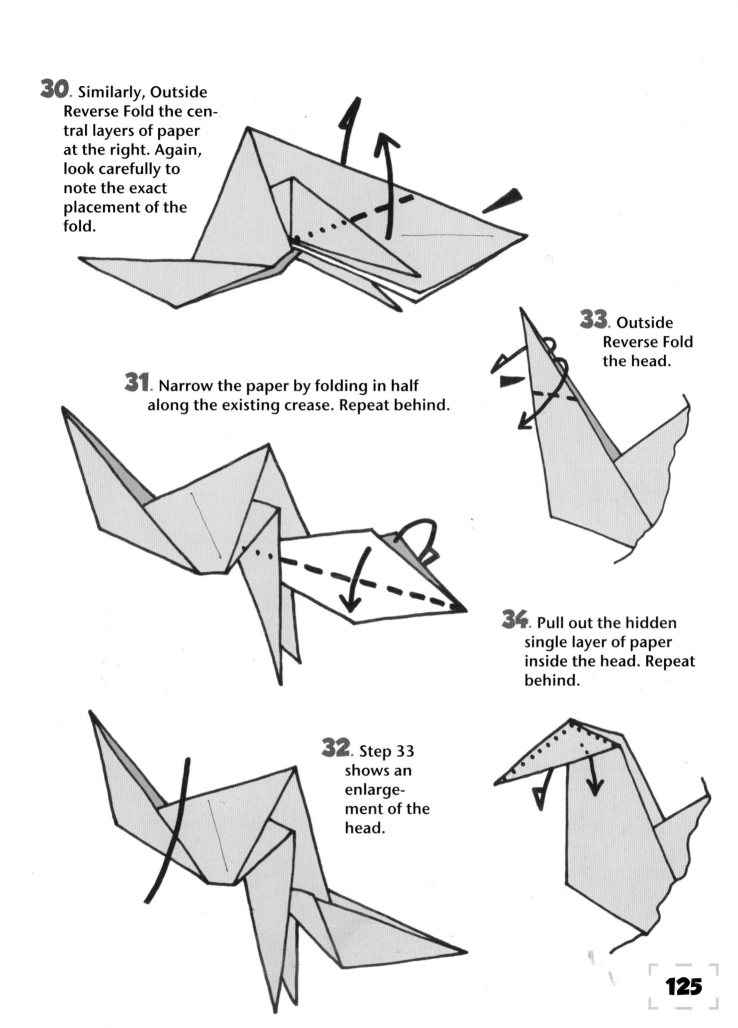

125

advanced

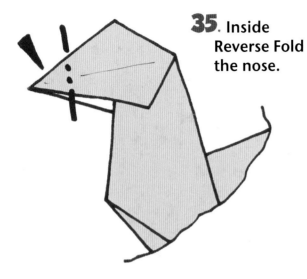

35. Inside Reverse Fold the nose.

36. This is the completed head.

37. Step 38 shows an enlargement of the legs.

38. Inside Reverse Fold the foot . . .

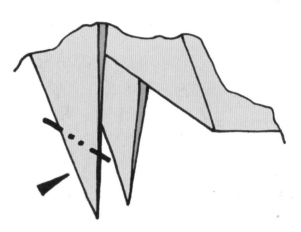

39. . . . then Inside Reverse Fold the foot again, to swing it forwards . . .

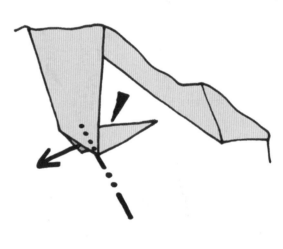

40. . . . like this. Repeat with the other foot, being very careful to fold it exactly the same as the first (or your model will stand lopsidedly!).

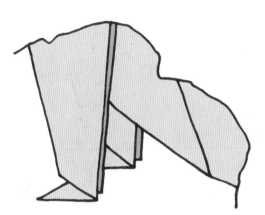

41. Step 42 shows an enlargement of the chest area.

42. Use scissors to cut along the thick line, then fold the fore-leg forward. Repeat behind.

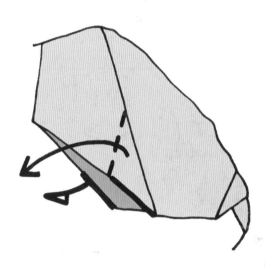

43. The Dinosaur complete. By adjusting the angle of the feet (Steps 38–39), the Dino will balance without resting on its tail as a third "leg." The tail fold itself (Step 30) may also need adjusting, so that it lifts clear of the ground.

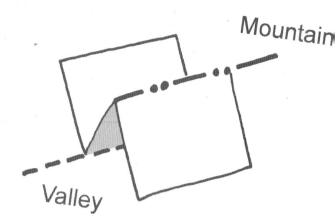

Mountain

Valley

Resources

You've folded the models in this book and now, of course, you want to learn more about origami. Here are a few suggestions for more folding fun:

The Internet

There are lots of excellent origami sites, and the list will doubtless continue to grow. Some feature a Web master's own work while others specialize in mathematical models, traditional models, geometric models, modular models, book reviews . . . and on and on. There are also many "how-to" origami videos.

Books

There are hundreds of origami books in print in many languages. Buying from the Internet on the basis of a cover photo and perhaps a few spreads can be very hit-or-miss. If you can, find unbiased online reviews before making your purchase. Better yet, visit a good bookstore or library. The universal system of diagramming used in this book means that if you really want that Japanese or Russian book you saw, you should be able to understand the instructions, even if you don't read the language.

Origami Organizations

Frankly, you can only learn so much online or from books. It's when you meet other people interested in origami that you learn more and enjoy it more. There are organized origami societies and clubs in many cities. To find a group, simply run a Web search on "origami." In the United States, the premier origami organization is Origami USA: www.origami-usa.org. In Britain, it is the British Origami Society: www.britishorigami.info.

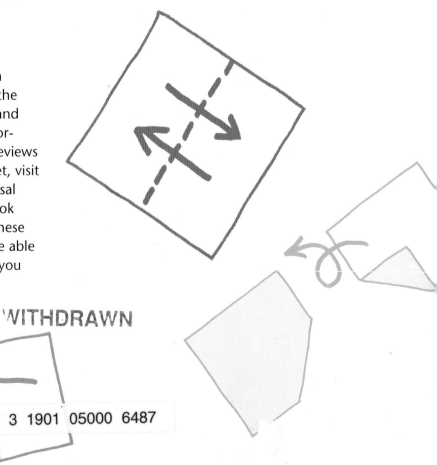